through the
eye
of the
needle

through the
eye
of the
needle

HOW TO EXPERIENCE the FULLNESS of CHRIST

CHARLES T. DAVIS

Through the Eye of the Needle:
How to Experience the Fullness of Christ

Published by DEVOTION PUBLISHING
Edmond, Oklahoma
Copyright ©2018 CHARLES T. DAVIS. All rights reserved.

No part of this book may be reproduced in any form or by any mechanical means, including information storage and retrieval systems without permission in writing from the publisher/author, except by a reviewer who may quote passages in a review.

All images, logos, quotes, and trademarks included in this book are subject to use according to trademark and copyright laws of the United States of America.

Library of Congress Control Number: 2018931972
DAVIS, CHARLES T., Author
Through the Eye of the Needle
Charles T. Davis

ISBN: 978-0-692-99204-3

RELIGION / Christian Life / Spiritual Growth
RELIGION / Christian Ministry / Discipleship

QUANTITY PURCHASES: Schools, companies, professional groups, clubs, and other organizations may qualify for special terms when ordering quantities of this title.
For information, email Info@DevotionPublishing.com.

All rights reserved by CHARLES T. DAVIS
and DEVOTION PUBLISHING.
This book is printed in the United States of America.

This book is dedicated to Christians worldwide. God called me to write this message to followers of Christ. *Through the Eye of the Needle* is truly a work of the Lord for the growth and transformation of Christians. As God has brought my heart more into alignment with His, He has given me an increasing compassion to help Christians experience the living Christ. My prayer is that out of each reader's transformative practice in reading this book, he/she will gain an increased passion and desire to share and disciple others in understanding all that Christ has to offer.

Bibles Versions Used

HOLY BIBLE, NEW INTERNATIONAL VERSION ®
Copyright © 1973, 1978, 1984 by International Bible Society
Used by permission of Zondervan Publishing House.
All rights reserved.

THE NEW AMERICAN STANDARD BIBLE.
Copyright © 1960, 1962, 1963, 1968, 1971, 1972, 1973, 1975, 1977, by
The Lockman Foundation.
Used by permission. All rights reserved.

NEW REVISED STANDARD VERSION
Copyright © 1989
Division of Christian Education of the National Council of the Churches
of Christ in the United States of America.
Used by permission. All rights reserved.

The Holy Bible, English Standard Version® (ESV®)
Copyright © 2001 by Crossway,
a publishing ministry of Good News Publishers.
All rights reserved.

CONTENTS

Preface	9
Introduction	11
Chapter 1: Threading the Needle	17
Chapter 2: Where Am I With God?	51
Chapter 3: Making Your God Bigger	83
Chapter 4: Positioning for the Eye of the Needle	105
Chapter 5: What is Blocking Me?	131
Chapter 6: Going Through the Eye of the Needle with Heart	155
Chapter 7: Having the Will to Go Through the Eye of the Needle	177
Chapter 8: Stepping Through the Eye of the Needle	197
Chapter 9: On the Other Side	211
Appendix 1: Experiencing Christ - The Funnel	233
Appendix 2: Application - Feet for Applying God's Word	237
Appendix 3: Concordance of Topics	243
Special Thanks	249
About the Author	251

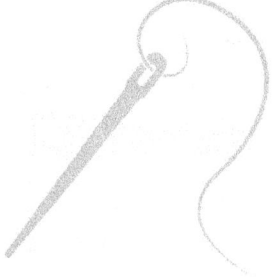

Preface

I AM NOT A WRITER, a church pastor, or an official in any Christian organization. I am simply a follower of Christ, responding to God's calling to write this book. This calling arose from the last Bible study I wrote called "Satisfaction." Satisfaction is a Bible study to help believers attain the satisfaction that God desires each Christian to experience. God has given me a message for the church, a gift for writing this book (with the help of countless friends), and a passion to help people not only know Jesus as their Savior and Lord, but also experience the living Christ.

This book was born from engaging with and discipling and witnessing to countless people for the last 47 years. My interactions discovered a common condition that is unfortunately increasing in an exponential manner with Christians. Christians are living their Christian lives often with no assurance that they are Christians, living without concrete knowledge of the eternal destiny of their family and friends, having no clear purpose of God's will, bearing little fruit in their Christian life, and dryly experiencing the Christian life. **Whether you are in none or all of these situations, God has more for you!**

God's desire for the salvation of all is only matched by God's desire for His love to be known and experienced by every person on this earth. I wrote *Through the Eye of the Needle: How to Experience the Fullness of Christ* to help Christians engage and experience Christ. You were saved to be more than an incubator of knowledge by attending church and other religious events. **God wants you to be a vessel of the Holy Spirit for His power in your life and others'.** You were saved to serve within the church and to be an ambassador of God's love outside the church by serving and ministering to others. God wants every person on this earth to experience His love and to abide in the exhilaration of knowing the living Christ.

My 47-year walk with Christ has given me a passion to help other Christians walk with Christ and experience Him and His promises. Your journey through this book will help you to understand what might be causing you to settle for less than what Christ wants you to have. It will also help you enter the abundant life that God desires for you. Each page of this book will be like peeling an onion. The more you read the more you will discover who you are in Christ while realizing the opportunity to experience more of Him. **Do not live another day without the passion desiring to live on the other side of the needle where Christ desires to express His life in and through you!**

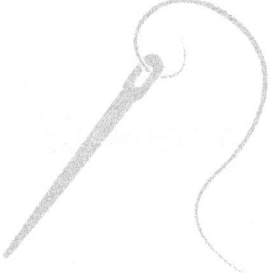

Introduction

Then Jesus said to His disciples, 'I tell you the truth, it is hard for a rich man to enter the kingdom of heaven. Again I tell you, it is easier for a camel to go through the eye of a needle than for a rich man to enter the kingdom of God.' Matthew 19:23-24 (NIV)

THROUGH THE EYE OF THE NEEDLE: How to Experience the Fullness of Christ is for all Christians, no matter where they are in their walk with Christ. This book seeks to pull back the curtain on **how you can experience the living Christ!** God did not redeem your life for salvation so that your best experience with Him is when He rescued you from darkness. Neither did Jesus die for you and impart new life only for you to fall away from Him because of a crisis of faith. Nor did God save you so that you could spend the rest of your life in Christ searching for answers, purpose, and direction.

Jesus came to earth, died, and rose from the dead for a threefold purpose: your salvation; your sanctification (becoming like Christ); and for you to bear fruit for Him as His ambassador. Bearing fruit is experiencing a little more of God as you respond to Him in obedience from hearing His truths and leadings. Christ wants to impart understanding, knowledge, and wisdom to better impart His direction in your life. The real question is, are you willing to slow down and give God the time to speak in and through your life?

Jesus has already answered the questions of your salvation, forgiveness of sins, and what is necessary for living the Christian life. These are settled issues that do not need to be ruminated on for the rest of your life; rather, they need to be acted on in obedience. **What requires your attention, devotion, and time is your sanctification in Christ, and God's mission for you as His ambassador.**

Christians are experiencing an ever-increasing disconnect between what their lives look like and the Christian life as Jesus promised in John 10:10: '...*I came that they might have life, and might have it abundantly.*' (*NASB*) The disparity in what God promises and what you are experiencing occurs primarily because you are not making Jesus Lord of every area of your life. You will seldom experience the living Christ in a classroom learning the do's and don'ts of Christianity. You will experience the living Christ out of the depth of your relationship with Him.

God did not save you to spend your life merely seeking His purpose, but as Lamentations 3:24 says, God desires to become your hope as you make Him Lord: '*The LORD is my portion,*' says my soul, '*Therefore I have hope in Him.*' (*NASB*) T*hrough the Eye of the Needle* will guide you in making God your portion so that God's will and purpose are more clearly known and worked out in you.

Jesus knew man's tendency to take control first then ask later for God's blessing and admiration. The rich man in Matthew 19:23-24

INTRODUCTION

was a perfect example of this by him asking Jesus how to gain eternal life. He thought he knew how to please God because of his efforts to fulfill God's commandments. He just needed a little affirmation and praise from Jesus for the great job he was doing. Instead, Jesus shocked him by quickly identifying the dark spot in his heart: money. What the man believed would be a coronation resulted in correction and despondency. The rich man's story is not unique. His plight was repeated while Jesus was alive and continues to be repeated by others today. In the quest to find satisfaction in life, nonbelievers are easily attracted to the beauty of the Christian message. While the life and message of Jesus reveals the simplicity of salvation in Christ, people obfuscate His message with their unwillingness to let go of self-centered priorities in life. This unwillingness comes from filtering the Gospel through your priorities, desires, and needs. Living this way begins to shut God out of your life by choosing your ways over God's eternal design.

Through the Eye of the Needle will take you on a journey of how you not only go through the eye of the needle for eternal life, but also how you go through the eye of the needle to begin to experience God's kingdom here on earth! God wants you to have an inner satisfaction that travels across all terrains of life with an eternal peace, joy, wisdom and perseverance. Job told his wife in Job 2:10 that God is alive and active in all conditions of life, *'Shall we accept good from God, and not trouble?'* (NIV) Finding God in good and difficult times requires more than a belief in God, but a sold out commitment. It is this kind of commitment that distinguishes a casual Christian from a disciple of Christ who follows Him wherever He calls. It is this type commitment that moves Christians beyond merely finding satisfaction in their relationship with Christ to accepting the call to be His disciple.

In Matthew 28:19, Jesus commands us to make disciples, *'Go therefore and make disciples.'* (NASB)

Jesus gave three attributes of disciples:
- Obeying the Word (John 8:31): *"If you abide in My word, then you are truly disciples of Mine."* (NIV)
- Walking in love (John 13:34-35): *"A new command I give you: Love one another. As I have loved you, so you must love one another. By this all men will know that you are My disciples, if you love one another."* (NIV)
- Bearing fruit (John 15:8): *"By this is My Father glorified, that you bear much fruit, and so prove to be My disciples."* (NASB) God wants to use you in bringing others into a saving relationship with Christ, discipling others, serving, and ministering.

Your life as a Christian is very similar to your physical journey as a human being. You entered this world as a baby, so will you enter your new life in Christ as a baby. God did not save you to remain a baby, but to grow to full maturity. In Matthew 19:21, which comes before the verse this book is based on, Jesus says,

'If you want to be perfect, go, sell your possessions and give to the poor, and you will have treasure in heaven. Then come, follow Me.' (NIV)

Another description of "perfect" would be "complete or mature." Paul challenged all Christians in Colossians 1:28: *Admonishing every man and teaching every man with all wisdom, that we may present every man complete in Christ.* (NASB) And again in Ephesians 4:13, Paul wrote:

Until we all attain to the unity of the faith, and of the knowledge of the Son of God, to a mature man, to the measure of the stature which belongs to the fullness of Christ. (NASB)

Introduction

It is this process of growing from infancy to maturity that you begin experiencing the life of Jesus in increasing measures. It is not an end result, but a continual process that blossoms and expands to allow you to experience and reflect more of the fullness of God. **As you grow in maturity your life will reflect more of the life and fullness of Christ** that is described in Ephesians 4:13. This is heaven on earth!

In Jesus' last days on earth, He spent time encouraging His disciples on how much better it would be with His departure. In John 16:7, Jesus explains why this would be better: *'But I tell you the truth: It is for your good that I am going away. Unless I go away, the Counselor will not come to you.'* (NIV) Why then do Christians have so much trouble going through the eye of the needle, considering how lavishly God has bestowed His grace on them, and how He has equipped each Christian? *Through the Eye of the Needle* strives to answer not only the "why," but the "how." The following chapters will help you understand those things that are hindering your transformation in Christ while exposing you to more of Jesus' life and works as well as the work of the Holy Spirit.

Ephesians 1:18-22 gives you a beautiful picture of what God wants you to experience:

> *I pray also that the eyes of your heart may be enlightened in order that you may know the hope to which He has called you, the riches of His glorious inheritance in the saints, and His incomparably great power for us who believe. That power is like the working of His mighty strength, which He exerted in Christ when He raised Him from the dead and seated Him at His right hand in the heavenly realms, far above all rule and authority, power and dominion, and every title that can be given, not only in the present age but also in the one to come. (NIV)*

Do not passively read this book, but aggressively engage God in the truths you are shown. Position your life to go through the eye of the needle, so that God can continue completing the reconciliation of your life to His that is described in Roman 5:10: *How much more, having been reconciled, <u>shall we be saved through His life</u>*. (*NIV*) I pray that as you go through the eye of the needle your heart, spirit, and life will be overwhelmed by the vast expanse of heaven that is waiting for you on the other side. Enjoy a walk with Christ that is far bigger than you ever imagined!

ONE

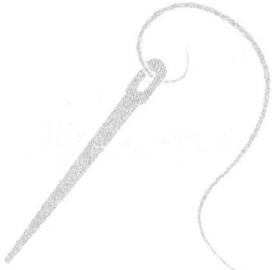

Threading the Eye of the Needle

IN PSALM 24:3 DAVID POSES two questions that have been asked a thousand different ways: *Who may ascend the hill of the LORD? Who may stand in His holy place?* (NIV) A very similar question was asked of Jesus after He told the rich man what he would have to do to go to heaven in Mark 10:27: *The disciples were even more amazed, and said to each other, 'Who then can be saved?'* (NIV) David and the rich man were seeking God, but both still wondered what was necessary to go to heaven. Both had their opinions. In Psalm 24:4 David answered his own question: *He who has clean hands and a pure heart, who does not lift up his soul to an idol or swear by what is false.* (NIV) In Mark 10:19, Jesus reminds the rich man of the Ten Commandments,

'You know the commandments: Do not murder, do not com-

mit adultery, do not steal, do not give false testimony, do not defraud, honor your father and mother.' The rich man answers Jesus in verse 20, 'Teacher,' he declared, 'all these I have kept since I was a boy.' (NIV)

Both men sought to better understand how they could improve their standing with God. We know a lot about David, but we know little about the rich man. Yet the answers of both men indicate their hearts not only desired God, but that they also pursued God. God was important to them; He was essential in their lives, but both longed to experience Him more intimately.

Just as David and the rich man desired relationship with God, so people today desire to know and experience God. God places this innate need in every person's life. The desire to know and experience God is different than actually pursuing, hearing, and responding to God. The quest that Christians have for God feels quite differently today than during the time that David and the rich man lived.

Today's Christians do not seem as focused on dwelling with God. Instead they are more focused on their needs: paying the bills, having the right job, dealing with conflicts, handling depression, and having healthy relationships. Christians today appear to be perpetually seeking God's will and how to get out of the mud pits of life rather than seeking to live in the center of His will. The identity of our Christian faith has shifted from knowing and experiencing more of God to being comfortable in the Christian institutions of church, Bible studies, small group, worship groups and occasional ministry. Today's Christian might be better defined by finding a reasonable compromise between the obligations of living life on earth and the Christian activities that meet their spiritual needs. This Christian lifestyle differs greatly from what Paul described in Romans 12:2: *Do not be conformed to this world, but be transformed by the renewing of your mind. (NASB)*

Paul saw the vibrant Christian life as a transformative experience that truly differentiated a Christian from a non-Christian. The Christian life is not about meeting minimum expectations or developing a spiritual routine, but a transformed life that intimately knows Christ and lives all out for Him. This follower of Christ is known not by what he says or what he does on Sunday morning, but by a lifestyle that radiates Jesus. These Christians are not known by their Biblical knowledge, but by their love, joy, and peace. Their identity in Christ is not known by the church they attend but by their devotion and passion for God. This lifestyle only comes from consistently going deeper into a committed, loving relationship with Jesus.

Stephen in the book of Acts beautifully portrayed a follower of Christ who was not only transformed, but also knew Jesus intimately. Stephen's life did not portray minimal Lordship where he followed God only when it was convenient, but one who lived all-out for Jesus. Stephen could have prevented his own death by turning away from Jesus, but this was not an option for him. The Sanhedrin condemned Stephen for his faith and actions. They believed his faith so abhorrent to their faith that they were going to kill him. Yet in Acts 6:15, despite their animosity towards and intent to kill Stephen, they saw God's presence in his life: *All who were sitting in the Sanhedrin looked intently at Stephen, and they saw that his face was like the face of an angel.* (NIV) No amount of hate or disgust for his beliefs could deny the life of Jesus that showed in Stephen. **Whether others agree or disagree with you, do others see Jesus when they look at you?**

Christians are works in progress in their efforts to become like Jesus. Whether or not you become like Jesus will depend greatly on your devotion to Him. In today's Christian culture, it is easy to graze on the Christian faith by nibbling at what you like but rejecting what you do not like. A grazer tries to form God into his own image. Living your life in Christ this way will move you toward an impotent Christian experience.

God cannot transform, much less make fruitful, a Christian who has crafted God on their own terms. Christian churches are filled with Christians who are ineffectual for Christ. These Christians continually question God's actions, His ways, and the semantics of Scripture. Living your Christian life this way will leave you with many unfulfilled questions: Where is God's blessing? What is God's will? What is my purpose?

Living the Christian life by continually sifting truth to meet your needs can quickly devolve to spending most of your time battling the flesh (your desires), satan, and the world (what others and the culture expect and how they act), instead of experiencing God's abundance, provision, and purpose. Impotent Christians throw themselves at Christianity expecting God to perform. They have high expectations of God, but no spiritual root system to support those expectations. Their relationship with God is not exemplified by a desire to go deeper into Lordship (making God first) and intimacy with Christ. Instead, their relationship with Christ is filled with the expectation and desire for God to meet their needs. They love comfortable Christianity and its benefits but stop short when those benefits have a cost. Proverbs 19:2 describes such Christians: *Desire without knowledge is not good. The man in a hurry misses the way.* (*NEB*) You want your desires fulfilled, but are unwilling to pay the price. Your way of life does not leave room for God's desires. Psalm 51:16-17 describes one willing to pay the price:

> *You do not delight in sacrifice, or I would bring it; you do not take pleasure in burnt offerings. The sacrifices of God are a broken spirit; a broken and contrite heart, O God, You will not despise. (NIV)*

A gentleman I was discipling shared with me how the Christian group he attended had a member who was in a difficult financial situation. This person had lost his job and had been without work for some time. Two young children, a car and house payment along with all the daily needs had pushed his family to the brink of desperation. We discussed how he could give in this situation and how the group could participate. This gentleman said he would like to help, but his own family was barely making ends meet. I asked if he had asked God to show him anything his family should forgo, so that he could help this group member. The thought of sacrificing in order to give had not crossed his mind. How common this is. We tend to respond to life situations not out of God's resources and faithfulness, but out of our earthly construct of life.

It is easy to wear the banner of being a Christian, but when it comes to cost, hardship, and change, we often find convenient ways out. God did not save you for comfort, indulgence, and indifference, but to be His light and salt in this world. Proverbs 27:21 describes the navigation of hardships: *The crucible is for silver, and the furnace is for gold, and a man is judged by his praise.* (RSV) As a follower of Christ, you will often be placed in the crucible and furnace. How you respond to these circumstances reflects your faithfulness to God and your faith in Him to care for you.

This transitions us back to our original question on experiencing God — *who can ascend the hill of the Lord?* When the disciples heard Jesus tell the rich man what was required (for him this was like saying he could not enter heaven), they replied in Matthew 19:25, *'Then who can be saved?'* (NASB) Jesus answered their question by saying in Mark 10:27, *'With man this is impossible, but not with God; all things are possible with God.'* (NIV) What God asks of you is impossible on your own, but **what you can do with God in the power of the Holy Spirit is not only possible, but spectacular!** The rich man was clueless regarding his position with God. Likewise, many Christians are oblivious to their position in Christ. In Galatians 4:1 Paul describes it this way: *What I am saying is that as long as* *the heir is a child, he is no different from a slave, although he owns the whole estate.* (NIV) Every Christian is empowered to experience God's life and work, but they often live like a slave to the world, satan, and the flesh. They choose others, material things, and wrong paths that rob all that God has for them. Whether you are seeking God passionately like David, oblivious like the rich man, or more in the middle, you can experience more of God's work and presence.

Threading the eye of the needle is a figurative mindset that prepares you for going through the eye of the needle. Having a proper mindset for your relationship with Christ begins the process of laying a solid foundation for your Christian life. An analogy would be your computer. Your computer contains an operating system that allows all the other programs to operate. Without this programming, none of the other programs can operate properly. Proper programming for Christians includes beliefs that are grounded in the Word of God. The following are seven truths that are grounded in the Word of God, the bedrock of your faith. These seven truths create a firm foundation for threading the needle.

THREADING THE NEEDLE WITH GRACE

Grace is the foundational truth for Christians. Grace is God's unmerited gift that is offered to every human being for salvation, whether we deserve it or not — and none of us do. Salvation is God's gift of eternal life through the path He has provided. . .Jesus Christ. The impartation of salvation only occurs because of God's great love expressed by Christ's sacrificial death for our sins and His resurrection. Through God's grace, Jesus paid the price for the sins that separated us from God. Christ's redemptive sacrifice removed the penalty of death for sin while giving us the Holy Spirit, so that we can experience God. Despite God's grace, many Christians who have come into a saving relationship with Christ cling to corrupted beliefs that are not true.

Some common corrupted beliefs are:
- I must keep doing good works to have eternal life.
- God has not forgiven me for a terrible thing I did in the past.
- I failed again and do not deserve to have relationship with God, much less salvation.
- God cannot forgive me because of the type of person I am.

These corrupted beliefs have one common ingredient — they have bought into the lie that God's grace is not enough. They are based on the belief that your salvation is solely dependent on your actions and activities, not on God's grace. Such a mindset distorts the very essence of God's love and grace. Imagine a child going to bed every night wondering if his deeds and actions were enough to continue being the child of his parents. If you think something more is required for your salvation, then you undermine the foundational essence of Christianity, which is grace. Ephesians 2:8-9 proclaims God's grace:

For it is by grace you have been saved, through faith — and this not from yourselves, it is the gift of God — not by works, so that no one can boast. (NIV)

It is God's unconditional love that opens your heart to salvation and the process of sanctification. Sanctification is the process of becoming like Christ through the work of the Holy Spirit. Sanctification occurs through your belief and dependency on Christ, so that His life can be fully expressed in you. The mistake of constantly chasing after God's approval is in opposition to allowing His love to encapsulate your heart. Embracing God's grace and love allows Him to flood your heart with His life through the work of the Holy Spirit. God wants to go with you on your journey through life. You make this difficult when you have filled your "vehicle" with everything but God. Making God secondary as you continue to remain on the throne of your life leaves little room for God. Your good works and your struggles with believing in God's gracious love and forgiveness quickly consume any opportunity for God to take hold of and transform your life.

Receiving God's grace requires faith. It does not matter whether you consider yourself the worst of sinners or not a bad person at all. Both are sinners on the same level and both require the same payment for their sin to escape the punishment of death. Large or small, Jesus paid the price one time for all sin. In Matthew 20:15, in His parable of the day laborers, Jesus taught in a parable that all men receive the same compensation regardless of the hours worked, *'"Don't I have the right to do what I want with my own money? Or are you envious because I am generous?"'* (NIV) God is the One who has expressed His grace through the forgiveness of your sin, regardless of its severity. To receive and accept His grace requires two things, your faith and Lordship in Christ. God paid the penalty for your sin so that now, without any merit of your own, you can be reconciled to God. Your reconciliation with God requires you to accept, by faith, Jesus' sacrifice for your sins. Your step of faith to receive God's grace may stretch you, but God's love for you is the same regardless of the severity of your sin.m

God extends His love and grace equally to all. Unfortunately, the freedom and power of His love and grace can be received unequally. God's forgiveness of your sins occurs through His atoning sacrifice in Jesus. The atoning power of God's grace is dependent on nothing you earn but can be affected by your recognition of sin. Your faith to accept God's forgiveness and grace will be fueled by the depth of your recognition of sin and your repentance from it. Until you realize the depth of your brokenness, it will be difficult for you to need Jesus. In Luke 7:47 Jesus teaches how an increasing recognition of sinfulness enlarges faith,

'Therefore, I tell you, her many sins have been forgiven — for she loved much. But he who has been forgiven little loves little.' (NIV)

In other words, the depth of your repentance will help take you into the depths of God's grace and love. Recognizing your need for God allows the Holy Spirit to change the sinful areas of your life. Your failure to believe God's forgiveness and receive His grace usually results from failing to recognize your sin and your need for forgiveness. This results in shallow repentance. Shallow repentance is receiving Christ with little recognition of your sin and need for forgiveness. Areas of sin not recognized exclude God's work. You fail to submit these areas to God out of disobedience or lack of recognition. Becoming a Christian does not require every sin to be confessed. However, receiving Christ with little recognition of your sin and no heartfelt conviction of the sinner you are keeps Christ at arm's length. Christ may now be in your heart, but the character traits that make fertile ground for sin in your life go virtually unchanged. Shallow repentance is the quencher of the Holy Spirit. Shallow repentance disbelieves or easily rejects God's love and grace. The freedom God intended for you is still trapped in an unrepentant nature that struggles to make Christ Lord.

It is important for a follower of Christ to fully embrace Christ's work on the cross. Recognizing not only your need for Christ, but also your brokenness, will enliven you to the work of the Holy Spirit. You must continually allow the Holy Spirit to work in your heart, so that your heart is sensitized to sin as well as freed from it. Sensitizing your heart to sin allows the Holy Spirit to sanctify you to become more like Christ. Allowing Christ to fully embrace your life by making Him Lord frees the Holy Spirit to work in you. Allowing God to do this transforms your life from the bondages of the flesh to living in the freedom of the Spirit. By continuing in shallow repentance, you allow the weakness of your flesh to undercut your faith, preventing God's transforming work. This results in a life that is constantly questioning God's love and ways. Shallow repentance undermines the tremendous inheritance that has been bestowed on you, while fully embracing God's unmerited grace allows God's full work in you. Colossians 1:13-14 shows the power of God's grace: *For He has rescued us from the dominion of darkness and brought us into the kingdom of the Son He loves, in whom we have redemption, the forgiveness of sins.* (NIV)

THREADING THE NEEDLE WITH CHILDLIKE FAITH

The second truth for threading the needle is not only to receive Christ with childlike faith, but to live through Him with a childlike faith. Jesus took the opportunity in Luke 18:16 to instruct His followers not to hinder the children from coming to Him. He continued in Luke 18:17 to teach that the mental and emotional condition of a child is fertile ground for receiving the kingdom of God' *'I tell you the truth, anyone who will not receive the kingdom of God like a little child will never enter it.'* (NIV) People often seek God with so much baggage that they make it difficult for God to touch their hearts for salvation. People like this try to develop logical explanations concerning faith to help them make a faith decision. They work to understand the historical reality of Christ so that they can believe with confidence that Jesus was not a hoax. They study the Bible to assure themselves it makes sense and is true before they believe. People have all types of reasons for not believing, including other people, parental examples and their quality of experiences in religious settings. My favorite one is, "I would never become a Christian, because if there was a God, He certainly would not have allowed this to happen." This person's disbelief is predicated on his belief of how God should be! "I believe, therefore God should be this, and if You are not what I believe You should be, then You cannot be, and I cannot believe." If you got lost reading that logic, I assure you I got lost writing it!

The need to have a childlike faith must have floored many of those listening to Jesus. Many in Jesus' audience began early in life rigorously training and learning the Torah (the first five books of the Old Testament written by Moses), memorizing Scripture, following all the customs and traditions, and meticulously following the law. It was this type of life and activity that got people to heaven, not the childlike faith Jesus taught. **This truth is powerful in a Christian's life because it is not by knowledge that you will know Christ, but by becoming totally vulnerable to Him.** Jesus wanted people to come to Him with no preconceived beliefs. Becoming a Christian in this manner means your knowledge is secondary and your faith becomes primary. This path to salvation prevented people from wrapping Jesus around their belief systems. In 1 Peter 1:8, Peter defined the importance of this kind of faith:

Though you have not seen Him, you love Him; and even though you do not see Him now, you believe in Him and are filled with an inexpressible and glorious joy. (NIV)

Jesus taught those listening to accept Him by faith rather than processing who He was by logic, by the world's thinking, or by what the world deemed as acceptable.

A child does not have the problem of wrapping Jesus around a preconceived belief system, because a child's world is not yet formed. A child's filter is minimal and can easily accept new truths as reality. A child's filter does not block the Holy Spirit's leading, instruction, and conviction, but allows the Spirit to freely speak into his or her life.

Receiving Christ for salvation while holding so many caveats explains why it is so easy for some Christians to have shallow repentance and nominal faith. After all, it takes time to form God into your image! Fortunately, our God does not bend to our desires, but continues to work and speak His truth into our lives. You see this principle at work in Hebrews 4:12:

For the word of God is living and active. Sharper than any double-edged sword, it penetrates even to dividing soul and spirit, joints and marrow; it judges the thoughts and attitudes of the heart. (NIV)

Another important attribute of children is that they are not entrapped by the world; they are pliable and available. Adults live in straightjackets that filter every life commitment through schedules and available time, while children change on a dime. Making Jesus Lord as an adult is easier said than done, but children do not have to pay bills, be at work, and tend to their responsibilities. In the eyes of a child, if it looks good, do it. The more we describe the difference between a child and an adult, the more you recognize the impact of what Jesus was teaching. His teaching was radical. No wonder Lordship is said and declared more than done and lived.

This is a pivotal truth for going through the eye of the needle. You cannot be wrestling in the 100-pound category while you weigh 200 pounds unless you are willing to drop weight. In the same way, if you want Jesus to be Lord in deed and not just in proclamation, you must be willing to make changes to allow God to work in your life. You make this happen by not making God merely an accessory that can be fit into your schedule; allowing yourself to have margin; making God a priority and not an interruption; and making your lifestyle secondary to God. Making Jesus Lord allows Him to not only touch your heart, but also work in your life. I met a gentleman a few months ago for lunch. As I walked in, he was just finishing his meal. I asked why he did not wait. He said he liked to arrive early and leave late to be available to engage people. He said he prayed daily for divine encounters, which God frequently arranged. To do this, he had to leave margin in his schedule. This lifestyle takes a new mindset, a heart that craves God, and a devotion to fall in love with Jesus. Jesus taught this reset of the mind in Mark 2:21-22,

> 'No one sews a patch of unshrunk cloth on an old garment. If he does, the new piece will pull away from the old, making the tear worse. And no one pours new wine into old wineskins. If he does, the wine will burst the skins, and both the wine and the wineskins will be ruined. No, he pours new wine into new wineskins.' (NIV)

This changed mindset does not depend on your skills, knowledge, and efforts. Instead, it comes by asking Jesus to take control of your life, show you the way, teach you His ways, and give you a heart that yearns for Him instead of things of this world.

THREADING THE NEEDLE WITH RIGHTEOUSNESS

The third truth is righteousness. Did I really say that dirty word? We are made righteous at salvation. Righteousness means right-standing before God. God made Jesus, who had no sin, to be sin for us, so that we might become the righteousness of God. Jesus took our sins (past, present, and future) to the cross and exchanged our sins for His perfect righteousness so that we can one day stand before God, who will not see our sins, but only the holy righteousness of the Lord Jesus. I am saved by grace and therefore made righteous, but wait, don't I still sin? Romans 3:21-22 proclaims our righteousness:

But now a righteousness from God, apart from law, has been made known, to which the Law and the Prophets testify. This righteousness from God comes through faith in Jesus Christ to all who believe. (NIV)

How then can I be righteous, but still sin?

I grew up having no confidence because I believed I was intellectually inferior to others. I had the distinction of failing first grade. In second grade I had to wear an eyepatch and thick horned-rimmed glasses. In third grade, my front tooth was knocked out in baseball and replaced with a silver cap. All through elementary school, I had mediocre grades and was resigned to my inability to make good grades. In seventh grade, something happened that changed my life. On my first report card, I had 3 C's and 3 B's. My mother mailed copies of my report card to every person she knew. My first thought was horror from the embarrassment this would bring. However, this act brought a much different result, because my mother included a letter praising me for my good grades. I was uplifted, but amazed. If I could get that type of praise for those grades, think what I could get for better grades!

At that point in my life, I received a new nature (secularly that is, in the area of intelligence). I began to apply my new intellectual nature more diligently in my education, which resulted in even better grades. The same is true spiritually. 2 Corinthians 5:17 describes you as a new creation when you become a Christian: *Therefore, if anyone is in Christ, he is a new creation; the old has gone, the new has come! (NIV)* The sovereign Lord described your new heart and spirit in Ezekiel 9:13, *'I will give them an undivided heart and put a new Spirit in them; I will remove from them their heart of stone and give them a heart of flesh.' (NIV)*

Your life is now primed and ready for transformation to become like Christ in the sanctification process. When I realized I had the ability to do well in school, I still had to make myself available for it to happen. I still had to do the things that were required for good grades. The same is true spiritually. At salvation God not only made you a new creation and gave you a new heart and Spirit, but He immediately began opening His heart to you. The opening of God's heart began revealing unrighteousness (continuing to sin) in your life. God uses this revelation of unrighteousness to woo you to righteousness through the work of the Holy Spirit. Any negative response to God's leading will be a roadblock in the sanctification process. The Holy Spirit is leading you to sanctification, but will you obey? Are you willing to displace those blockers (anything that blocks God's sanctifying work) in your life for God's righteousness? Yielding to God allows His righteousness to be cultivated through the Holy Spirit.

Your transformation only comes from God through the work of the Holy Spirit. The work of the Holy Spirit will only happen as you go deeper into your relationship with Jesus. Out of the depth of your relationship with Jesus, you will start to be transformed to the point where your heart and mind will say, like David did in Psalm 17:15: *And I — in righteousness, I will see Your face; when I awake, I will be satisfied with seeing Your likeness.* (NIV) This transformation of your heart and mind will cause you to love righteousness more and more. Your love for righteousness will start to provide visible changes in your life that will bring happiness, satisfaction, and a desire for more. Your desire for righteousness will start to become like a snowball going down a mountain, becoming bigger with each roll. This is when the truth of righteousness no longer brings a groan or a blind eye, but instead an expectant smile at what God will do with each step of faith toward Him in righteousness.

Paul describes this growing love for righteousness in Philippians 1:11 as the fruit of righteousness: *Be filled with the fruit of righteousness that comes through Jesus Christ.* (NIV) The fruit of righteousness occurs as your growth in Christ hungers and thirsts for more of God's ways. In previous struggles with God, you fought to hold on to things that were contrary to God. You now readily embrace and accept what God has for you. These struggles now become life experiences that amplify the benefits of Godly living and God's work in you. **Your willingness to die to self (place God's ways before your ways) and leave everything behind allows God's life in you to produce the full bouquet of His righteousness in you.** Psalm 146:8 gives a good visual picture of this: *The LORD lifts up those who are bowed down, the LORD loves the righteous.* (NIV) When you submit to God's ways and direction, the Lord lifts you up. God's love for you, like a parent for a child, overflows with joy as righteousness flows more freely from your life. As you go further in this reading, you will learn multiple facets of falling more in love with God's righteousness.

THREADING THE NEEDLE – MAKE JESUS LORD

The fourth truth is Lordship. The rich man was only willing to go so far in making God Lord of his life. He was willing to make God Lord over his honesty, his marital faithfulness, his truthfulness, and his not bearing false witness, but when it came to money, Matthew 19:24-25 showed he had other plans: *Jesus looked at him and said, 'How hard it is for the rich to enter the kingdom of God!'* (NIV) Psalm 66:18 illustrates how not making Jesus Lord robs you of the life God desires for you: *If I had cherished sin in my heart, the Lord would not have listened.* (NIV)

The rich man was not willing to make God Lord over his money; for you, it might be relationships, ministry calling, negative character traits, or placing vocation above God and family. Is there any area you are holding back from God or trying to find satisfaction outside of God? **What you are seeking, satisfaction apart from**

God, demonstrates your indifference and pride in not needing God. This indifference and pride quenches the work of the Holy Spirit.

Allowing God to be Lord in every area of your life invites Him to satisfy every area of your life. You place God first because you love Him more than anything else. You allow God's control because you know nothing satisfies more than Him, His perfect ways, and the fruit born from it. Your world has become God's kingdom. **You on your throne has been replaced with God's total habitation of your life. Your desires have become what God desires, because nothing satisfies like Him.**

THREADING THE NEEDLE BY KNOWING HIM

The fifth truth is relationship with Christ. Nothing will happen in your Christian walk outside of your relationship with Christ. The more vibrant your relationship with Christ, the fuller your life will be. A superficial relationship with Christ will leave you with a deficit in your walk with Him. Your walk with Christ represents how you interact and live with Christ. A dryness in a Christian's walk with Christ can almost always be explained by a superficial relationship with Christ. Your pursuit of knowing Christ better will result in a richness of relationship that yields great rewards, while a superficial relationship with Christ will result in a dry, unfulfilling experience that brings little satisfaction. Jeremiah 17:7-8 beautifully illustrates the pursuits and the rewards of relationship with God:

> *But <u>blessed</u> is the man who <u>trusts</u> in the LORD, whose <u>confidence</u> is in Him. He will be like a <u>tree</u> planted by the water that <u>sends out its roots by the stream</u>. It does <u>not fear</u> when heat comes; its <u>leaves are always green</u>. It <u>has no worries</u> in a year of drought and <u>never fails to bear fruit</u>. (NIV)*

Jesus took this truth a step further on the cross. Jesus magnified the power of your relationship with God in John 17:3 when He said, *'Now this is eternal life: that they may know You, the only true God, and Jesus Christ, whom You have sent.'* (NIV) Jesus defined eternal life as knowing God. We cannot begin to understand the fullness of eternal life from this statement, but **Jesus clearly saw His relationship with God as the ultimate experience in life.** What better way of emphasizing the importance of your relationship with God than by describing it as the indescribable experience of eternal life: Not just in the future, but right now, here on earth! If you place this experience as the ultimate, then logically **anything that will happen in your Christian experience will flow out of your relationship with God.**

The opportunity of experiencing eternal life here and now should provide a powerful motivator to better know God and build a deeper relationship with Him. Experiencing God begins by connecting with God. Connecting with your loving Father can happen on multiple fronts, but some are more important than others. Having a personal "quiet time" each day where you are giving God dedicated, uninterrupted time to allow communication in prayer and Bible reading is one of the first steps to experiencing God. You continue your connection with God throughout each day as you engage Him with the details of your life. As an employee at work constantly engages his supervisor for direction, inspiration, and growth, in the same way you must constantly engage your heavenly Father throughout the day. Do you pursue God's Words in your life? God will be impressing His Word in your life, if you are having a regular quiet time and continuing to engage Him throughout the day. Engaging and pursuing God allows Him the opportunity to speak into your life. Here are some of the ways Jesus modeled this truth during His typical day:

Luke 6:12: One of those days Jesus went out to a mountainside to pray, and spent the night praying to God. (NIV)

Mark 6:46-47: After leaving them, He (Jesus) went up on a mountainside to pray. When evening came . . . (NIV)

Luke 4:42: At daybreak Jesus went out to a solitary place. The people were looking for Him and when they came to where He was, they tried to keep Him from leaving them. (NIV)

John 6:15: Jesus, knowing that they intended to come and make Him king by force, withdrew again to a mountain by Himself. (NIV)

Mark 1:35-36: Very early in the morning, while it was still dark, Jesus got up, left the house and went off to a solitary place, where He prayed. Simon and his companions went to look for Him, and when they found Him, they exclaimed: 'Everyone is looking for You!'(NIV)

There is nothing small about experiencing the eternal life Jesus mentioned in John 17:3. Allow the magnificence of this opportunity to capture your heart. Allow yourself to know Jesus more intimately and passionately to such a degree that He becomes a consuming fire in you. **Let God's passionate fire and love flow out of your consuming love for Him. Rejoice and enjoy the eternal life that God intends for you to experience today.**

THREADING THE NEEDLE - TRANSFORMATION

The sixth truth is Transformation. God saved you to be an image bearer of Christ. "But I thought we were saved to glorify Him?" You cannot glorify God to others or Himself without the transformative process of becoming more like Christ. The number one reason people reject Christ is they do not like what they see in Christians. Do you want the lost, who are on their way to hell for eternity, to be saved? Then allow God to transform your life in such a way that they see, hear, and experience the love of Jesus through you. Do you want a good marriage and children who are Godly to succeed? Allow God to transform your life in order that Jesus can be real to them. Do you want your culture to be Godly? Then allow God to transform your life to such an extent the culture not only sees Christ in you, but also sees a picture of what our world can look like.

One reason children do not come to Christ in salvation, or reject their faith, is due to parents who do not live out their faith. Parents must not only know Christ, but also be living examples of God's transformative work. Children who see God's active work in their parents are drawn to God. The power of representing Christ was illustrated by a friend of mine. My friend shared how seeing her earthly father live his Christian life reinforced her belief in God her heavenly Father. She shared that a friend asked her, "How can you have so much faith in God? I just wish I had your faith." The woman replied,

> "God's unconditional love for me has never been a question. My faith in God as my Father has always been real because of the example of my earthly father. It made sense that my heavenly Father would love me no matter the circumstances. My heavenly Father would never let me down, because of the example of my earthly father. My earthly father's ex-

ample never made me question his intentions towards me. I have a friend whose earthly father abandoned her mother and her as a child. Her father to this day is not dependable and does not show her love. My earthly father has loved me and been dependable, which resulted in a stronger trust in God, my true Father. My earthly Father set the foundation for me to fully depend on God as I grew in my relationship with Him. Because of my earthly father's reliability, it only made sense to trust God because He is the only real thing in this world. My friend has only known misplaced trust and felt the need to perform for her earthly father, which has always been followed by rejection and feeling nothing is stable and true. This is a trend that can be seen over and over. This false belief is beaten by the truth that God, the better Father, will never leave you, and always desires His best for you."

As you can see from this story, your testimony as a Christian impacts your family, friends, and the world. The world often translates who God is by your Christian example.

In Romans 5:10 you see how God wants to transform His people into the light and salt of the earth: *For if, when we were God's enemies, we were reconciled to Him through the death of His Son, how much more, having been reconciled, shall we be saved through His life!* (NIV) God wants every Christian to experience life abundantly here on earth. You experience this life through Jesus. It is Jesus who transforms you for abundant life through the process of sanctification, which is becoming like Christ. Sanctification is like breathing. First you breathe in through Bible reading, prayer, meditation, and waiting on God. Then you breathe out by trusting God, stepping out in faith, believing His promises, and obeying Him. **Living this way allows the One who saved you for eternity to also save your life on this earth by His life.**

You can thwart the transformative process of sanctification by resisting where God is taking you. Consider the illustration of a child reaching into a jelly bean jar trying to pull out as many jelly beans as possible. It was easy to insert an empty hand into the jar, but impossible to extract a hand full of jelly beans. If you continue to hold onto multiple desires that are not of God, it will be difficult for God to transform your life. **As you breathe in, God will speak into your life. When God speaks you must breathe out by responding and letting go of that which thwarts God's purposes.** This frees you to breathe out by not only hearing, but by also responding and releasing those areas you have been clinging to that block God. This allows God to take over in order for you to experience the life He desires for you. The deeper you go into relationship with Jesus, the greater your sanctification, resulting in greater transformation. **Let go and let God.** As you walk with God, let Him speak into your life as Paul admonished Timothy to not miss the life God had for Him in 1 Timothy 4:16:

> *Pay close attention to yourself and to your teaching; persevere in these things; for as you do this you will insure salvation both for yourself and for those who hear you. (NASB)*

Paul did not want Timothy and those around him to miss the glorious riches of God's abundant life. Neither do you!

THREADING THE NEEDLE BY GROWING TO MATURITY

The seventh truth is that God wants you to grow to maturity. Every truth to this point contributes to your maturity in Christ. Spiritual maturity does not happen randomly but is an intentional process that occurs brick-upon-brick. You have met many adults in life whom you judge to be immature. Their immaturity is marked by inconsistency, lack of responsibility, and unnecessary hardships from poor choices. The same is true for an immature Christian. Are you actively applying God's truths and leadings in your life? Are you consistent in the disciplines of spiritual growth? Are you obedient to God's Word? You can act "Christian" while being inconsistent in pursuing Christ, negligent in taking hold of what God puts before you, and knowingly disobedient. God wants you to grow to maturity not only to experience the riches of the life He has for you, but also to be a picture of the kingdom of God. Mark 4:30-32 illustrates Jesus' desire and the results of growing to maturity:

Again He said, 'What shall we say the kingdom of God is like, or what parable shall we use to describe it? It is like a mustard seed, which is the smallest seed you plant in the ground. Yet when planted, it grows and becomes the largest of all garden plants, with such big branches that the birds of the air can perch in its shade.' (NIV)

God desires every Christian to grow to full maturity for others to see a living picture of the kingdom of God. In 2 Corinthians 3:2 Paul encourages the Corinthians to live their lives in Christ in such a way that anybody can know about Christ by seeing Christ in them: *You yourselves are our letter, written on our hearts, known and read by everybody.* (NIV) Consider the end of the parable of the sower, *"with such big branches that the birds of the air can perch in its shade."* This illustrates how God wants your growth in Christ to be not only a picture of who God is, but to also provide support and covering for others. Maturity in Christ goes beyond studying the Bible, attending religious activities, and talking about what you hear; it also requires you to allow God to transform His truths into action. 1 Corinthians 4:20 challenges Christians to respond to and obey the truths they are confronted with, so that more of God's work and power can be released in them: *For the kingdom of God is not about talk, but power.* (NIV) Your maturity in Christ will take you into a deeper and richer experience of His kingdom on earth. Your maturity will show others the character, majesty, and love of God as you provide opportunities to support the body of Christ while serving and ministering in the world.

YOUR FOUNDATION

Matthew 7:21-23: 'Not everyone who says to Me, "Lord, Lord," will enter the kingdom of heaven, but only he who does the will of My Father who is in heaven. Many will say to Me on that day, "Lord, Lord, did we not prophesy in Your name, and in Your name drive out demons and perform many miracles?" Then I will tell them plainly, "I never knew you. Away from Me, you evildoers!"' (NIV)

As instrumental as knowing these seven foundational truths in threading the needle, knowing Jesus Christ as your Lord and Savior is ground zero. Knowing Jesus Christ as Lord and Savior is the strong box that not only holds these seven truths together, but it also empowers them. Without a conversional experience with Christ you may risk two things: First, you may have become an institutional Christian who appears to have come to salvation in Christ but have not professed faith nor given your life to Him in Lordship. You participate in all or some of the recognized activities of Christianity, but you have never responded to the Holy Spirit's call to salvation in your life. Your participation in Christianity has become a macramé of good works laced over Christian traditions and activities. The writer of Hebrews 4:2 describes this Christian as follows:

For we also have had the gospel preached to us, just as they did; but the message they heard was of no value to them, because those who heard did not combine it with faith. (NIV)

The second risk is you know Christ as Lord and Savior, but your faith is sabotaged by corrupted beliefs. Corrupted beliefs are things you believe to be true but are not. Living and acting on false truths can keep you from experiencing and acting on "The Truth." There are many reasons corrupted beliefs can undermine your salvation in Christ. Not having a clear conversional experience can make it easy for corrupted beliefs to hinder your walk with Christ. Not being discipled or taught the truths of salvation opens your life to wrong doctrine, false teachings, non-Biblical rules, experiences that distort your belief system, and sin that has caused you to distort God's truths. These corrupted beliefs are landmines waiting to crater a believer's life.

Prayerfully and carefully read the following message of salvation to have assurance of salvation and to clear up any corrupted beliefs. If you are already a Christian and confidently walk in the faith, take this time to better train yourself on the Gospel message so that you can comfortably and boldly present the gospel to those who are not Christians. The security of who you are in Christ not only solidifies the seven foundational truths, but also further energizes Christ's work in you.

There is an interesting truth for Christians hearing the gospel message that is connected to going through the eye of the needle. Christians can grow in knowledge where they think they are beyond the need of the Gospel message of God's grace. The reality is that you are never beyond need of God's grace. Mature Christians hunger for deeper levels of the Gospel message as the love of Christ penetrates their lives. Becoming numb to the gospel shows a need for going deeper into Christ to experience more of His wonder, grace, and love.

THREADING THE NEEDLE - SALVATION

Here are a number of corrupted beliefs; Christians with these kinds of beliefs are constantly blocking God in their lives.

CORRUPTED BELIEF
"There are multiple ways to God." "God's truth is flexible to accommodate non-Biblical beliefs."
TRUTH
You cannot make yourself the arbiter of truth. God alone is the originator, gatekeeper, and arbiter of truth. John 14:6 shows us there is no salvation in anyone else when *Jesus stated, 'I am the way and the truth and the life. No one comes to the Father except through Me.'* (NIV) There is only one path and one way for salvation. For mankind to be saved, God had to provide the perfect sacrifice for your sins by the death and resurrection of Jesus. Jesus' sacrifice is God's provision for your sin. You can add nothing to God's provision for man's salvation. Ephesians 2:8-9 reminds us that it is by God's grace alone that we can be saved through faith: *For it is by grace you have been saved, through faith — and this not from yourselves, it is the gift of God— not by works, so that no one can boast.* (NIV)

CORRUPTED BELIEF
It is not necessary to acknowledge your sinfulness.
TRUTH
Romans 3:23 declares that we all are sinners: *For all have sinned and fall short of the glory of God.* (NIV) You are a sinner that falls short of the holiness of God. Your sin separates you from God, and there is nothing you can do to bridge this chasm. God is Holy; He

requires you to be holy. Romans 6:23a tells us: The wages of sin is death. (NIV) This is a spiritual death which means an eternal separation from God. God revealed in the Old Testament that only a blood sacrifice could temporarily pay the price for sin. But these blood sacrifices were never enough because the sacrificed animals were not perfect. God sacrificed His perfect Son on the cross (shed His blood) to cover your sins and pay the price for your sins so that you can live eternally with God. Jesus' sacrificial death meant He took your sins upon Himself to pay the complete price for your sins with His blood. Failure to repent from the sin in your life could lead you to intellectually commit to Christ while not truly letting Him into your life. Brokenness and acknowledgement of known sin is the doorway to repentance and salvation, while pride and love of sin can be powerful blockers of allowing the Holy Spirit to redeem your life for salvation. **Your salvation is not a negotiation with God, but a surrender to His life and will.**

CORRUPTED BELIEF
Hell and separation from God is not real.
TRUTH
Hell and eternal separation from God is not a fantasy or something that can be avoided through any manipulation of man. Sin is sin. The wages of sin is spiritual death from God and unchangeable. Psalm 100:3 proclaims: *Know that the LORD is God. It is He who made us, and we are His; we are His people, the sheep of His pasture.* (NIV)

Romans 6:23 declares the consequences of not knowing Jesus as your Lord and Savior: *For the wages of sin is death, but the gift of God is eternal life in Christ Jesus our Lord.* (NIV) Eternal death and separation from God occurs with those who have not come into a saving relationship with Christ. The precursor to coming into a saving relationship with Christ is acknowledgement of your sinful nature and accepting your need for God.

CORRUPTED BELIEFS

These are two related corrupted beliefs.

1. You refuse to accept the reality that God can love you for who you are. Your mindset about your past life, inadequacy, and undesirableness makes it impossible for you to accept the fact that God not only loves you for who you are, but that He also loves and accepts you the way you are.

2. You cannot accept the fact that Christ's sacrificial death paid the price for your sins. You believe that the horrendous nature of your sins are unforgiveable. Your unbelief in God's unconditional love and grace causes you to continually come back to God for forgiveness, redemption, and salvation.

TRUTH

John 3:16 gives the clear path to salvation: *For God so loved the world that He gave His one and only Son, that whoever believes in Him shall not perish but have eternal life.* (NIV) Recognizing and receiving God's love, sacrifice, and forgiveness opens your heart to receive Him into your life. Believing Jesus died for your sins and placing your faith in Him to be Lord of your life results in salvation and eternal life. Belief involves the recognition of your need for God and God's provision in Jesus for that need. Placing your faith in Jesus is the transfer of your ownership to Him as your Lord and Savior.

CORRUPTED BELIEF

Christ's death and resurrection are inadequate to pay the price of your sins. You believe your sins require your special effort and actions for salvation. You doubt God's provision for salvation by rejecting His death and resurrection as the payment for your sins. You are constantly working for God's approval.

TRUTH

John 1:12 gives the action steps to becoming a Christian: *Yet to all who received Him, to those who believed in His name, He gave the right to become children of God.* (NIV) You are a child of God when you believe in Jesus Christ as God's provision for your sin and you ask Him into your life as Lord and Savior. You not only believe He took your sins and paid the price, but you also receive Him as the new owner of your life.

CORRUPTED BELIEF

You believe that more is required for your salvation. This belief causes you to be the one who produces righteousness instead of God. You live your life in Christ fearing you must do more to please Him. Your corrupted belief says your acceptance and ultimate salvation requires your vigilance to perform for God's approval.

TRUTH

Romans 10:9-10 describes the action steps of salvation: ***That if you confess with your mouth, 'Jesus is Lord,' and believe in your heart*** *that God raised Him from the dead, you will be saved. For it is with* ***your heart that you believe*** *and are justified, and it is with* ***your mouth that you confess*** *and are saved.* (NIV) Through faith, you believe in God's provision for salvation. God sent Jesus as a sacrifice for your sins and raised Him from the dead in order that you might have eternal life. With your mouth, you proclaim Jesus as Lord of your life. You submit every part of your life to Jesus as the Lord of your life. Faith and confession releases the full manifestation and power of your new life in Christ.

CORRUPTED BELIEF

You believe you are inadequate or disqualified for salvation and from having a relationship with Christ. You start to accept lies that encumber and deactivate God's promises. Accepting these lies constantly puts God in the closet of your life, so that you experience less and less of the fruit of the Spirit. Instead of believing as

John the Baptist when he said, **"He must increase, but I must decrease,"** you say, "I must do more, so I can have more of God."
TRUTH

Rebuke the thief and embrace Christ who loves you. In John 10:10, Jesus declares God's desire for you to experience a rich life in Him, *'The thief comes only to steal, and kill, and destroy; I came that they might have life, and might have it abundantly.'* (NASB) Jesus provides life, while satan, the ways of the world, and your flesh stand ready to rob your life of the abundant life God has for you. Every choice going forward will be a choice for either the thief to steal the abundance God has planned for you or to allow God to give you the abundance and peace He desires for you. You have life eternally and can have life now in Christ. With your every breath, decision, and action choose Jesus - not the thief.

CORRUPTED BELIEF

You believe you can lose your salvation. This means believing God can abandon you as His child, that God is not true to His Word, that He can revoke His promises and you can never have the confidence of God's love for you. This discouraging existence puts you in constant doubt and fear.
TRUTH

1 John 4:18 reaffirms there is no validity in this fear, because God is love and His love is perfect, trustworthy, and eternal: *There is no fear in love. But perfect love drives out fear, because fear has to do with punishment. The one who fears is not made perfect in love.* (NIV) Jesus did not die on the cross so that you would spend the rest of your life looking over your shoulder. Jesus paid the price for your sins. He wants you to spend the rest of your life looking forward to eternal life with Him and what He has for you. John 5:24 and Romans 8:38-39 affirms your eternal security (you can never lose your salvation) in Christ:

John 5:24: 'I tell you the truth, whoever hears My word and believes Him who sent Me has eternal life and will not be condemned; he has crossed over from death to life.' (NIV)

Romans 8:38-39: For I am convinced that neither death nor life, neither angels nor demons, neither the present nor the future, nor any powers, neither height nor depth, nor anything else in all creation, will be able to separate us from the love of God that is in Christ Jesus our Lord. (NIV)

Your salvation in Christ is a done event that assures you eternal life with God. You are no longer condemned to death for your sins but have passed from death to life. There is nothing in all creation that can separate you from Christ. There is no need to doubt or question God because He has given you every assurance of salvation and eternal security for your peace of mind.

This book is written to help Christians experience a full and vibrant life in Christ. Christ desires not only your salvation and eternal life, but also a transformed person who lives in His power and presence every moment. It is out of this relationship with Christ that you will experience all He has for you as a faithful and fruitful follower. To continue reading this book without clearly knowing you are fully reconciled with Christ in salvation would be a fruitless exercise. If you have any doubt where you stand with Christ, clear that up now without spending another moment outside of the full assurance of salvation God desires for you. This is one decision you want to be clear on, because it involves your eternal destiny. This is one decision you do not want to procrastinate on, because you have no assurance that tomorrow will come for you. At that point your eternal destiny is locked in. Since everything in your Christian life will flow out of your relationship in Christ, you must know with certainty that you are a Christian for this to happen.

You can know with certainty that you are in Christ by believing and professing the following:

- Recognize and accept you are a broken, fallen individual who is a sinner before God and are in need of Him.
- Repent of your sins and ask God for forgiveness.
- Recognize your need for God not only because of your sin-condition, but also for your very existence. Peace and satisfaction can only come from God your Creator.
- Believe in the person of Jesus Christ: His life, death, and resurrection paid the price of your sins; His desire is for you to be His child through your profession of faith.
- Turn over your life to God. Ask and allow Jesus Christ to be the Lord of your life. Commit from this point forward you will live your life under Jesus Christ' will and direction.

If you believe these things and are ready to place your faith in Jesus Christ as Lord and Savior, please pray the following prayer:

Lord Jesus, I am not worthy of Your grace by anything I have done, but only because of the ultimate sacrifice You made in dying for my sins on the cross. Thank You for loving me enough to die for me. Thank You for paying the penalty for my sins. Thank You for making Your salvation available through Your wonderful gift of grace that is extended to me by Your death and resurrection. I ask that You come into my life as my Lord and Savior. Cleanse me of my sins, fill me with Your Spirit, and take control of my life. In Jesus' name I pray, Amen!

If you sincerely, through the transformative power of the Holy Spirit, prayed that prayer for the first time, or you were moved to nail down once and for all your salvation, *you are saved*! You will never again need to make this profession of faith. Nothing can separate you from God. You are God's child. His purpose for you is for your protection, growth, and maturity in Christ. God wants to fully establish your life in Christ in order that you better understand how to connect and grow with God. A good Bible study to help you do this is "Your Life in Christ" from the Growing in Christ website at www.growinginChrist.net . If you made this profession of faith for the first time, I would like to gift you "Your Life in Christ." You may request your free Bible study by emailing Charles T. Davis at charlestdavis@cox.net. I will send you your free Bible study along with a free weekly devotion that will help you in your new life in Christ.

Once you establish yourself in the faith, God wants to equip you to be fruitful in your Christian walk. An effective study for this would be "Discipleship" at the Growing in Christ website. Whether you already know Christ as your Lord and Savior with full confidence of who you are in Christ, or you just accepted Christ for the first time, or you solidified your salvation through a reaffirmation of your faith, you are now fully ready to go through the eye of the needle, **so that you can experience the full wonder and power of Christ on the other side of the needle!**

TWO

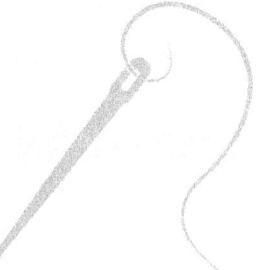

Where Am I with God?

THERE ARE SEVERAL REASONS JESUS lived, died, and was resurrected. One of those reasons is so that you may have abundant life. Christians are not meant to live in spiritual poverty but in joy, peace, and spiritual empowerment. Spiritual empowerment is the life that flows from experiencing Christ. The life of a Christian is not intended to mirror the world, but to throw off a pleasing fragrance to attract those in the world to what God offers - a life with God that brings meaning and fullness. Too often we hear stories of Christians whose lives do not draw others to Christ, but often repels them.

Here are some stories of such Christians that I have encountered:
- A Christian couple who came from Christian homes were married as Christians with vows of commitment for life. Within two months they were separated, with their mar-

riage eventually ending in divorce.
- Another Christian couple had been married for two years. They too were married as Christians with vows of commitment for life. The husband was frequently enraged while the wife repeatedly attacked and emasculated him. They worked on their marriage, but would give and take enough to find peace. They divorced after a child and four years of marriage.
- A man who is 33 years old became a Christian at six. He lived in a Christian household. Over the years, he drifted from the Lord and recommitted multiple times. He currently is in his fifth drug rehab center.
- A man had known Christ since age seven, grown up in a Christian home and walked faithfully with Christ. For many years, this man struggled with pornography. He tried to break free but continued to live in the bondage of sexual perversion.
- A child was born into a Christian family. At age eight, he accepted Christ. He went to church every Sunday and faithfully participated in church youth programs. He rejected Christ early in his freshman year of college.
- A man who professed Christ became embittered with the early death of his wife. He rejected Christ because he believed a loving God would never have let his wife die.
- A man who professed Christ most of his life eventually left the church and practices his faith in the seclusion of his own life. He has no spiritual interaction with other Christians. He became a Christian recluse because of the way other Christians treated him.

These are some examples of Christian failure instead of Christian abundance. Instead of Christ transforming lives to be a compelling attraction for others to come to God, many Christian lives have been beset with devastation and abandonment of God. Many of the negative statistics that reflect our society differ little in the lives of Christians. One of the harshest statistics is suicide. The essence of a Christian is life with hope and purpose, yet suicide rates for Christians differ little from non-Christians. While the causes of suicide are often rooted in the temporal things of this world, a Christian's life should be rooted in one's eternal hope in Christ. How can a person born again in Christ while possessing the Holy Spirit end his life in such despair? Another sad statistic is that 75 percent of young people leave the church after high school. If young people are experiencing the living Christ by graduation, they should be drawn into greater commitment and mission for God rather than indifference. How can young Christians have Christian parents, go to church, be involved in Christian activities, and not experience a loving and caring God who has a plan for their lives?

Christians who experience these results are reflecting the disconnect they have with God. Some type of disconnect with God probably exists in varying degrees with all Christians. These create a sandy foundation upon which believers base their lives. A disconnect from God usually begins with corrupted beliefs or areas of compromise that have allowed sin into the believer's life. Stepping back and allowing God to search your heart will allow God to reveal some of the areas where you might have built your life on a sandy foundation. God wants your faith to be built on His truths instead of the temporal things of this world.

The failures and bondages Christians struggle with often point to less-visible sin that goes unattended. Consider the development of sexual impurity for a married man. He may be comfortable viewing light porn in movies and magazines and enjoy fantasizing about other women. On the surface there is no visible harm. Beneath the surface, the heart is not only being compromised, but also hardened against the work of the Holy Spirit. This unapparent sin is a wreck waiting to happen. Less visible sin often flourishes and contributes to the sprouting of new sin conditions. In the previous example, it can be stepped up pornography consumption, more personalized sexual encounters, or adultery. Sexual impurity, other sin conditions and corrupted beliefs can bring significant struggles into a Christian's life.

Christians spend a lot of time struggling with temptation and fallout from a compromised life in sin while ignoring the root causes that create fertile ground for sin to flourish. Accepting Christ is an incredible rebirth, but unless you position yourself for His life and work, you will miss much of the life God has for you. It would be no different than getting married but living separate lives. Yes, you are married, but unless you engage in your marriage, you miss its purpose and benefits. **Understanding where you are will help you understand who your God is.** Is God piloting your life, or is He constantly working on you in the intensive care unit? Diagnosing your underlying beliefs will help you identify any corrupted beliefs that are sabotaging your walk with Christ. Replacing these corrupted beliefs with proper Biblical truths will free you to live in the power and presence of God.

The following eleven positions will help you understand where Christ resides in your life:

POSITION 1 – KNOWING CHRIST AS SAVIOR

Chapter 1 ended with the importance of knowing Jesus as Lord and Savior as well as rooting out corrupted beliefs that are affecting your relationship with Christ. My personal story picks up here. I never had any incident that brought me face-to-face with God for salvation. However, I experienced a gradual, uninformed process that left me with uncertainty. In my church I was perceived as a Christian while not being a Christian. I went to church almost every week for 16 years but did not know what a Bible was. My minister held me out as a Christian, yet Christ had no place, impact, or hold on my life. At age 16, circumstances caused me to question who God was. This led me to finding salvation in Christ over the next two years. I am grateful that God never abandoned me but continued to woo me to Him in His own ways. My story—being a part of a church but not knowing Christ—is not unique. Christian churches make it easy for the unsaved to blend in, participate, and become some of their most prominent members. Our culture makes it easy to participate in Christian institutions and activities whether one is a Christian or not. We easily bestow God's promises on people when we have no idea of their eternal destiny with God. Doing this sets up non-Christians to blame God for the circumstances of their lives even though they have never come into a saving relationship with Christ.

Life is filled with people in spiritual turmoil, destructive lifestyles, serious life circumstances, and relational conflicts requiring help and support from others. One of the first questions I ask when talking to one concerned about someone in these circumstances is where that person stands in knowing Jesus Christ as their Lord and Savior. Eighty percent of the time, the person does not know where their spouse, child, sibling, friend, or a person of significance stands in their relationship with God. Sixty percent of the time they say they think they know Christ. Think so?! How often do you make a life and death decision with "I think it will work?" Would you want to occupy a skyscraper where the contractor "thinks" the proper foundation was laid? Why would we live with the uncertainty of not knowing the single most important decision in a person's life? We shouldn't.

There is nothing more destructive than one living as a Christian without knowing Christ as Savior. In Revelations 3:15-16 God describes the importance of knowing your eternal destiny,

> *'I know your deeds, that you are neither cold nor hot. I wish you were either one or the other! So, because you are lukewarm — neither hot nor cold — I am about to spit you out of My mouth.' (NIV)*

Non-Christians living as Christians have become so prevalent today that when Christians live the Christian life, they are ostracized as hypocrites. The world has come to expect worldly lives from Christians. The world's expectation and definition of a Christian has transitioned from what Jesus and the Bible say to what pseudo-Christians say and how they live. Look at the press reaction to people who make decisions based on their faith and the word of God concerning their opposition to same-sex marriage. Newscasters were astounded that people could be so hypocritical, bigoted, and mistaken in their beliefs. Newscasters could not understand how anyone who called themselves Christians could reject this slice of our politically-correct culture.

Early in my walk with Christ in 1972, as a young youth director, I attended a local divinity school for training and equipping in the faith. I was stunned to hear these ministers talk. Their thought processes were not driven by the word of God; they were crafting culturally-acceptable positions that appeased the world. At that time, I was memorizing Scripture and had just done a significant amount of memory work in Romans. During a vigorous discussion on homosexuality, I used Romans 1 to challenge the prevailing acceptance of homosexuality in the group. The Scriptures were totally discounted. These ministers had long forgone their use of the word of God as their guide.

When you try to live like a Christian outside of God's truth, you are missing the power and beauty of Christianity. What a miserable existence it would be to try to live the Christian faith as a philosophy. In Matthew 7:21 Jesus states this clearly,

> 'Not everyone who says to Me, "Lord, Lord," will enter the kingdom of heaven, but only he who does the will of My Father who is in heaven.' (NIV)

The power of Christianity is Christ living in you. The difference between Christianity and other religions is that in Christianity, the God of the universe reveals Himself, His ways, and His path to life now and for life eternal. Life now and eternal life are determined by God's choosing, not ours. In Luke 13:23-27 Jesus shared a parable describing the sad ending for someone who based his life on a philosophy instead of the living Christ:

> …Someone asked Him, 'Lord, are only a few people going to be saved?' He said to them, 'Make every effort to enter through the narrow door, because many, I tell you, will try to enter and will not be able to. Once the owner of the house gets up and closes the door, you will stand outside knocking and pleading, "Sir, open the door for us." But He will answer, "I don't know you or where you come from." Then you will say, "We ate and drank with You, and You taught in our streets." But He will reply, "I don't know you or where you come from. Away from Me, all you evildoers!"' (NIV)

A firm understanding of who you are in Christ and how you got there moves you from living a philosophy to living a life that connects with Christ. It is this link with Christ that opens the door to the Holy Spirit transforming and empowering you. Receiving Christ with the faith of a child takes you through the narrow door. Once through the door of salvation, be careful not to neutralize who you are in Christ by filtering truth through the brilliance of your thinking or by qualifying truth with the ways of the world. Psalm 147:10-11 emphasizes God's desire for you:

His pleasure is not in the strength of the horse, nor His delight in the legs of a man; the LORD delights in those who fear Him, who put their hope in His unfailing love. (NIV)

Fully embrace and celebrate God's great love and provision for your salvation. Do not live your life in Christ like it is a smorgasbord of options, but fully devote your life to Him. Galatians 2:20 teaches you to allow Christ's life to become your life:

I have been crucified with Christ and I no longer live, but Christ lives in me. The life I live in the body, I live by faith in the Son of God, who loved me and gave Himself for me. (NIV)

Ask yourself, "Where am I?" "Is Jesus my Savior?" "Do I believe God's promises and walk in them?"

POSITION 2 – WHO'S ON BASE?

There is a fine line between Christ living His life through you or living it in your own strength. You can begin living your life through Christ by His Spirit, but quickly morph to where there is no Christ; there is only you. Living the Christian life through your human efforts tells God you do not need Him. Paul admonished the Galatians in Galatians 3:3 to stay under the yoke of Christ: *Are you so foolish? After beginning with the Spirit, are you now trying to attain your goal by human effort?* (NIV) Most Christians are unaware that their largest struggle in living the Christian life is allowing Christ to live His life through them. Christians focus on the issues affecting their lives while the root cause of these issues is not allowing Christ to be in control. This is why God says in Isaiah 66:2 that He loves those with a humble and contrite heart, '*This is the one I esteem: he who is humble and contrite in spirit, and trembles at My Word.*' (NIV) It takes humility to step down and allow God to take control of the throne of one's life.

It is important that you learn to walk in the Spirit, because much of sin, personal failure, and misdirection in life is a result of taking back control of your life from Christ. Walking in the Spirit is allowing Christ to live His life through you. This happens by spending time with God, hearing from God, and obeying. However, a Christian can totally obstruct this process or jump off along the way. My favorite Bible story on this is Peter walking on water. Peter saw Jesus and responded in obedience by getting out of the boat and walking on water. Peter was doing fine until he started looking at his circumstances which took his eyes off Jesus; immediately he began to sink. As Peter was sinking in the water, I can imagine him crying to Jesus, "How could you do this to me?" It was Peter, not Jesus, who changed focus. Peter lost his focus and trust when he took his eyes off Jesus.

Some time ago, I was dealing with a struggle and the Lord gave me a picture for keeping my eyes on Him. This picture is not pretty, but it is instructive. Jesus is holding me up on the end of a spear that is in my back. I am flailing and not liking my predicament. I want off because of my discomfort. God used this illustration to teach me that **I should stay on the tip of the spear**. My focus should remain on Jesus so that He can take me where He wants. I nicknamed this illustration "living on the tip of the spear." Walking in the Spirit is not always comfortable or pleasant, but it forces you to trust Jesus. Instead of getting off and doing it your way, you must continue to allow Jesus to take you where He desires. Continue to pray, read the Word, and respond to His calling as you endeavor to do His will while **believing that God's work in you will produce His best work**.

✞

Ask yourself, "Where am I?" "Am I leading, or is Christ?" "Am I allowing Christ to live His life through me?"

POSITION 3 – PURSUING JESUS

Jesus never promised that living the Christian life would be easy or convenient. Receiving all that God has for you requires perseverance and boldness. In Luke 11:5-8 Jesus gives a picture of pursuing Him in difficult circumstances:

> *Then He said to them, 'Suppose one of you has a friend, and he goes to him at midnight and says, "Friend, lend me three loaves of bread, because a friend of mine on a journey has come to me, and I have nothing to set before him." Then the one inside answers, "Don't bother me. The door is*

already locked, and my children are with me in bed. I can't get up and give you anything." I tell you, though he will not get up and give him the bread because he is his friend, yet because of the man's boldness he will get up and give him as much as he needs.' (NIV)

The man in this story received what he sought because negative circumstances did not stop him. Nor did the possibility of failure stop him. Neither did the prospect of a negative reception change his mission. Out of the depth of his conviction he boldly pursued what was needed, and he received it.

2 Corinthians 5:20a explains how Christians are on mission: *We are therefore Christ's ambassadors, as though God were making His appeal through us.* (NIV) Pursuing Christ on mission is not easy. As you pursue Christ, difficulties and sacrifices will reveal who you are in Christ. Who you are in Christ will illuminate the depth of your love for Him. The depth of your love for Christ will ultimately determine whether you will pursue Jesus to the finish line or end your pursuit of Him at your first challenge. Philippians 3:13b-14 shows how sacrifice, change, and the unfamiliar must be overcome in your pursuit of Jesus: *Forgetting what is behind and straining toward what is ahead, I press on toward the goal to win the prize for which God has called me heavenward in Christ Jesus.* (NIV) **Christ wants you to be impregnated with His mission.** Living a life that is permeated with Jesus will propel you deeper into Him rather than stopping short of the mission God has given you.

Ask yourself, "Where am I?" "Am I pursuing Jesus no matter the cost or effort?"

POSITION 4 – THE SOILS OF YOUR LIFE

Would a jury find enough evidence to convict you of being a Christian? Or would they declare you not guilty because they found you only an acquaintance of Christ and not one of His disciples? Would they find you not guilty because they found little evidence of you being a Christian? Christ wants to be such an important part of your life that others clearly see Him in you. Jesus described four types of Christians in Matthew 13:18-23,

> *'Listen then to what the parable of the sower means: When anyone hears the message about the kingdom and does not understand it, the evil one comes and snatches away what was sown in his heart. This is the seed sown along the path. The one who received the seed that fell on rocky places is the man who hears the word and at once receives it with joy. But since he has no root, he lasts only a short time. When trouble or persecution comes because of the word, he quickly falls away. The one who received the seed that fell among the thorns is the man who hears the word, but the worries of this life and the deceitfulness of wealth choke it, making it unfruitful. But the one who received the seed that fell on good soil is the man who hears the word and understands it. He produces a crop, yielding a hundred, sixty, or thirty times what was sown.' (NIV)*

The four types of soil described in this parable help you understand where you are in Christ. Each of these soils illuminates not only where you are, but also why you are that kind of soil. With which soil would you most identify with?

- Hard soil represents a heart that is not receptive to the work of the Holy Spirit. There is no pliability or desire for the things of God. God's truth is falling on a heart that is interested in God but not committed to Him.
- Rocky soil represents someone who has not allowed God's truth to go deep into his life, but merely tickle his ears. With any type of adversity, his faith quickly crumbles. He has done little to deepen his walk and faith in Christ. Hard times send this Christian to seek worldly solutions and support instead of God's help and assurance.
- The thorn represents someone who will not put God first. Instead, he focuses on things of the world. The world's appeal eclipses the reality and appeal of God. God's truth is quickly traded for the things of this world as a substitute for acceptance, comfort, and satisfaction. This Christian has not sought to deepen his walk and faith in Christ.
- Rich soil represents a heart and spirit that is fertile ground for God. God's Word is not only refreshing and transforming, but exciting. Rich soil hungers for all that God has, because there is nothing better. Adversity and temptation only drive this Christian to deeper levels of relationship with God. The life he lives in Christ allows him to experience more of God. These experiences with God create a hunger for more of God's promises and truths. The result is a harvest of righteousness that produces abundant fruit.

Every Christian probably has patches of each soil. Some Christians have excessive hard, thorny, and rocky soil while others have large amounts of rich soil that is taking them to deeper depths of availability and hunger for God. All Christians will experience seasons in life where their ability to bear fruit will vary. The key component in becoming rich soil is your desire and availability for God to till your life for a rich and abundant harvest. Are you willing to allow God to confront and eradicate sin in your life? Are you willing to put your hope and trust in God when times are difficult? Are you willing to allow the richness of God's love and grace to consume the things of this world? Romans 8:5-6 gives a strong word on how to be rich soil:

For those who live according to the flesh set their minds on the things of the flesh, but those who live according to the Spirit, the things of the Spirit. For the mind set on the flesh is death, but the mind set on the Spirit is life and peace. (NASB)

✟

Ask yourself, "Where am I?" "Am I good soil that is fertile for receiving and being all that Gods wants and has for me?"

POSTION 5 – BEARING FRUIT FOR GOD

Being fruitful for God is an integral part of growing in Christ and experiencing all that He has for you. I became a Christian by following through on a promise at age 16 to seek God. I was so ignorant of Christianity that I did not even know what a Bible was. I began by reading a prayer book thinking it was the Bible. Two years into this process, I sought counsel from the minister in the church I attended. The minister assured me I was okay and not to worry. This church did not believe in a conversional experience for salvation. Having no point of solidification of my faith caused me to not have assurance of who I was in Christ. In my quest for truth, the pastor answered my questions and uncertainties with a question. He asked me if I would be willing to be youth director of the church. Without a clear foundation of my salvation, and little Biblical knowledge or understanding of what the Gospel was, I accepted!

Whether I was a Christian at this point, I will never know. But within a year, Christ was in full control of my life. My course in life changed dramatically. The revelation of God's truth was life-changing, and my zeal for God was passionate. Out of sheer luck (mostly divine intervention), I began discipling three of the youth in my group by studying the book of John chapter by chapter. I did not know what discipling was but wanted them to grow as I was growing. Inadvertently I taught myself one of the first principles of discipling others: you only have to be one lesson ahead!

God used this process to impact their lives and mine. During the course of discipling these three youth, God unraveled truth in my life in such a transformative way that I was not just growing in Biblical knowledge, but I was bearing fruit multiple ways. My growth in spiritual maturity led me to disciple others, actively witness, work with the poor, and coach an inner-city sports team. Looking back, I firmly believe without that step of faith in trusting God by receiving and obeying the Word, God's full presence and work in me would not have been realized. By faith I trusted God and God was always faithful in His promises. I believe this is why Jesus said being fruitful was one of the three attributes of a disciple. In Luke 19:15-26, Jesus gave the parable of the talents which emphasizes the value God places on being fruitful by using what God has given you,

> *'He was made king, however, and returned home. Then he sent for the servants to whom he had given the money, in order to find out what they had gained with it. The first one came and said, "Sir, your mina has earned ten more." "Well done, my good servant!" his master replied. "Because you have been trustworthy in a very small matter, take charge of*

ten cities." The second came and said, "Sir, your mina has earned five more." His master answered, "You take charge of five cities." Then another servant came and said, Sir, here is your mina; I have kept it laid away in a piece of cloth. I was afraid of you, because you are a hard man. You take out what you did not put in and reap what you did not sow." His master replied, "I will judge you by your own words, you wicked servant! You knew, did you, that I am a hard man, taking out what I did not put in, and reaping what I did not sow? Why then didn't you put my money on deposit, so that when I came back, I could have collected it with interest?" Then he said to those standing by, "Take his mina away from him and give it to the one who has ten minas." "Sir," they said, "he already has ten!" He replied, "I tell you that to everyone who has, more will be given, but as for the one who has nothing, even what he has will be taken away." (NIV)

Bearing fruit is a fundamental trait of Christians who are flourishing in their walk with God. Within each Christian resides the Holy Spirit who is equipping and growing him for greater fruitfulness. In John 14:12, Jesus prepared His disciples for the things they would be doing when He departed,

> 'I tell you the truth, anyone who has faith in Me will do what I have been doing. He will do even greater things than these, because I am going to the Father.' (NIV)

You should not fear stepping out in faith to be used by God. In Philippians 2:13, you see how it is God and not you who produces fruit in your life: *For it is God who works in you to will and to act according to His good purpose.* (NIV) God asks only that He can use you in relationship to what He has allotted you. How God bears fruit will look different for every believer: a single mother, a childless couple, empty-nesters, a single Christian, a working Christian, one filled with relational skills, another with leadership skills, a person handy in the building trades, the elderly, and anyone who has experienced grief, divorce, addictions, being elderly or purity problems. God wants to use every Christian according to their gifting, position, and available time. **It is not how much you do or how great you are that matters but being a humble servant of God available for His use and purpose.**

My sister, who recently passed away, was a great testimony to the parable of the talents. Early in life she experienced trauma that mentally affected her. Despite her difficulties, she became a Christian. She faithfully followed God, going to church, reading the Bible, praying, supporting Christian ministries and connecting with people. She listened well, noticed well, then engaged people. Though different, she touched an amazing number of people. To my embarrassment, I did not recognize her gifting until her funeral. I assumed it would be a small funeral since she always lived alone and did very few outside activities. To my surprise, her service was filled with people who I never thought would attend. Time and again, people told me how nice she was and how much they enjoyed talking with her. They talked about how much they loved her. As I thought back, it became evident that who she was mentally allowed her to connect with others in a special way. Whenever I could not remember someone's name—which was always—she knew it and could tell me something nice about the person. She could easily engage with people by discussing their families and interests. What a gifting to have in a world that specializes in being impersonal: computerized calls, emails, texts, social media, and eating at the table in isolation as members text, talk on the phone, check messages, and play games. In the world's eyes she may not have had ten talents, but in God's eyes she used all her talents and more. **The talents you have are not nearly as important as how you allow God to use your talents.**

Being fruitful reflects much about your Christian life. The Christian life has four legs: salvation, intimacy with Christ, obedience and fruitfulness. Outside of salvation, none of the other three happen without involving all four. You cannot have intimacy with Christ without obedience and fruitfulness. Intimacy will call you to obedience and obedience results in fruit. Refusing to obey puts you at odds with God, which destroys intimacy with Him. Obedience apart from intimacy in Christ is walking in the flesh and not the Spirit. Living in the flesh will careen out of control, resulting in being fruitless. **Profitable fruit is born out of God's love, grace, and the work of the Holy Spirit.** Bearing fruit reflects a vibrant relationship with God that hears God and steps by faith into God's will. One who follows Christ in this way bears fruit thirtyfold, sixtyfold, and even a hundredfold.

Bearing fruit is God's sculpting tool in a Christian's life. Fruitfulness shows how much you believe in God by believing His truths. It then tests your faith by rejecting or obeying God's promptings. The fruit born from your obedience or disobedience will illuminate your faith walk in Christ.

- Real faith says, "I believe in heaven and hell and therefore I am willing to love someone enough to show them how to avert hell regardless of how it affects our relationship."
- Real faith says, "I believe that all things work for the good of those who love God regardless of the consequences."
- Real faith says, "It is not about right or wrong, but forgiveness."
- Real faith says, "I do not have to react to an offense by someone else. I choose to trust God and go forward."

Bearing fruit tests your obedience by using the gifts and opportunities God puts before you. **Your response to God leading you in areas of being fruitful will become the pottery tools that He uses to shape and mold your life.** God uses all circumstances for growing in Him, whether He is exposing sin in your life, growing you in spiritual maturity, or using you as His hands in the life of another.

Just as Christian parents should aim to raise Godly children, I think God uses children to mature His adult children in the faith. Children can act as a sculpting tool in helping parents grow in developing Godly character and selflessness. Raising children can quickly reveal character flaws and shallow spirituality. Children call you to redirect your self-centered life to one that is other-centered. In the same way, God's work in you allows you to experience God, but also allows God to take you further into His purpose.

Bearing fruit is the meeting of knowledge and application (action). A Christian whose faith consists of an abundance of activities to impart greater spiritual knowledge becomes vulnerable to stagnation. Knowledge without the application of the truths produces little growth or fruit. **However, knowledge that is followed by obedience will bear fruit and result in greater growth and intimacy in Christ.** Imagine a brain surgeon who keeps reading and studying the brain to learn how to perform surgery, but never does surgery. You go to him for surgery and are impressed when he proclaims himself the world's greatest brain surgeon even though he has never performed a single surgery. He is very knowledgeable, but he has had no practical experience. No amount of knowledge will bear out his proficiency as a surgeon. The same is true spiritually. You can read and study vast amounts of Scripture, but until you place yourself in the hands of God for His use, you will be stagnant in your faith. If you want to grow and become fruitful, you will have to become the living sacrifice Paul describes in Romans 12:1:

Therefore, I urge you, brothers, in view of God's mercy, to offer your bodies as living sacrifices, holy and pleasing to God — this is your spiritual act of worship. (NIV)

You will deepen and strengthen your relationship with God every time the Holy Spirit pulses through your life, producing fruit through obedience. In John 14:21 Jesus explains how God manifests Himself to those who obey:

"Whoever has My commands and obeys them, he is the one who loves Me. He who loves Me will be loved by My Father, and I too will love him and show Myself to him." (NIV)

✠

Ask yourself, "Where am I?" "Am I hearing and obeying God so that I can bear fruit?"

POSITION 6 - COMPLACENCY

Bearing fruit in the life of a Christian is often thwarted by complacency, which can look like this: You know Christ as Lord and Savior. You have a good church and are connected with like-minded Christians in a group or with personal friendships. You have found a comfortable rhythm for spiritual growth through quiet time, Bible study group, or personal study. You found a place to serve and even contribute to a ministry. God is working in your life personally and in the lives of others. This is a wonderful place to be, but **the comfort of where you are can quickly replace the active work of God in your life.** You are spiritually active, but are you interactive? Are you hearing, experiencing, and responding to God?

In John 15:1-2 Jesus tells how God deals with complacency,

'I am the true vine, and My Father is the gardener. He cuts off every branch in Me that bears no fruit, while every branch that does bear fruit He prunes so that it will be even more fruitful.' (NIV)

Those who heard Jesus say this must have been shocked. I remember the first time I read this verse, I thought, "What does God want?" What I have come to understand is how much higher God's ways are than mine. My best will always be short of God's best. My obedience will be corrupted by my flesh. It is easy for God's journey in a Christian's life to become like laying immovable railroad track. Your Christian walk can become an end in itself, where your Christian activities become your relationship with God.

God's transformative work in you naturally occurs as a by-product of God's life in you. As your character, obedience, and love for people and God grow, God's work in your life will grow and change. **Not growing and experiencing God can put His plans for you on hold until your walk with Him catches up.** God cannot take you any further than you are making yourself available. Another aspect of not growing in your walk with Christ is stagnation. Stagnation is dangerous because **a Christian life without growth is a Christian life that is dying.** Complacency and all that surrounds it has taken over and becomes your God. It is no longer God directing and enlivening the steps you take in life, but your routine. Your comfort level has risen to the point where God is irrelevant. Your Christian life continues as always regardless of what God has for your life.

A vibrant Christian whom I discipled for several years went through some life changes. These changes created good excuses for dropping many of the spiritual disciplines that had fed his walk with Christ. Difficult times often require adjustments, but dropping or adjusting the wrong things can have negative consequences on your relationship with God. His quiet times went from six a week to maybe one on a good week. He was no longer journaling what God was speaking or doing in his life, probably because he was unavailable to God—or not listening. His Scripture memory, which was based on major impressions in his life from God, were now zero. His witnessing and discipling dropped off the map. He did have areas that trended upward. The staleness of his relationship with God was off the charts. His marital conflict was up. His job dissatisfaction was very high. He was experiencing increased depression.

I always find it amazing that for some reason, many Christians react to difficult times by dropping God. When this happens, complacency has already infected your relationship with God to the point that it is dead or on life support. Your response to difficultly shows that you do not believe in a living, personal God that lives in you, but that your belief in God is so shallow that it evaporates at the first signs of trouble. If you lose your relationship with God during difficult times, it's because you do not have a passionate, growing relationship with Christ. The living Christ in you has been reduced to rules, guidelines, and spiritual activities done as a duty rather than love for the Savior Himself. **Difficult times should drive you more into the hands of God, not away from Him.** Your response to difficult times should not diminish God's presence in your life but provide greater opportunities for further growth in your relationship with Him.

The perfect, infinite, unimaginable God is always speaking into your life. His Word will challenge your comfort zones, as well as your love for Him. "I love my group of friends." "I love where I work." "I love being able to drive this car." These are all great, but sometimes God has something greater. I wonder if Paul was responding to the temptation of complacency when he wrote Galatians 2:20:

I have been crucified with Christ; it is no longer I who live, but Christ who lives in me; and the life I now live in the flesh I live by faith in the Son of God, who loved me and gave Himself for me. (RSV)

It had to be far more comfortable for Paul to stay in Ephesus than to face the emperor in Rome. In Ephesus he was having ministry success and the church in Ephesus was growing. Why go to an unknown and possibly hostile environment? Because God called Him! **Paul was pliable to change because he loved God more than himself.**

God continues to cultivate the fruit in your life for even better fruit. You must never allow complacency to replace God's work and will in your life. **God will be constantly taking you deeper into Him for a richer experience while producing a more bountiful harvest, if you are available, pliable, and willing.**

✝

Ask yourself, "Where am I?" "Am I enlivened to the Spirit enough to allow God to prune me?" "What area is God currently pruning, growing, and changing?"

POSITION 7 - RIGHTEOUSNESS

Righteousness is right standing with God. Righteousness reflects God's character and life. Psalm 11:7(a) puts righteousness in perspective: *For the LORD is righteous, He loves righteousness.* (**NKJV**) As you grow closer to God, you will grow in righteousness. This is another great barometer for the depth and intimacy of your relationship with Christ. Is righteousness growing and expanding, or is there constantly the battle of right and wrong? Righteous living is an outgrowth of your relationship with Christ. Righteousness in your life should not be like fingernails on a chalkboard, but like sandpaper smoothing and crafting wood. In the beginning it is rough, but as you continue it becomes smoother and smoother. **In the beginning God's work in you can be difficult and unpleasant, but over time it becomes more pleasing and enjoyable as righteousness becomes a natural part of His life in you.**

A Christian's life will become increasingly receptive to righteousness. As your heart, mind, and spirit are transformed by the Holy Spirit, your actions gladly choose righteousness over the ways of the world. Every step of righteousness allows you to experience a little more of God. 2 Timothy 2:22 describes the process of righteousness:

Flee the evil desires of youth, and pursue righteousness, faith, love and peace, along with those who call on the Lord out of a pure heart. (NIV)

A Christian must literally flee evil for God to take him or her into righteousness. As the transformative process in Christ continues, you begin to pursue righteousness more than you flee evil. **You no longer see righteousness as a drudgery, something you have to do or an outdated contradiction to life; you see it as an ever-expanding portal into God's heart.** Righteousness is not a drudgery, but a joy. Romans 12:21 is instructive in this process: *Do not be overcome by evil, but overcome evil with good. (NKJV)* The flesh, the ways of the world, and acts of satan will be consumed by God's increasing righteousness in you as you walk with God in the power of the Holy Spirit.

Ask yourself, "Where am I?" "Is my heart being more drawn to righteousness than the things of this world?"

POSITION 8 - LORDSHIP

I was having a vibrant discussion with a friend about his rejection of Christ for salvation. You could tell he had discussed this many times before. He was artful in telling me why he was not a Christian. He laid out multiple reasons, most of which had to do with his priorities, the way he lived, and the desires of his life. I left saddened that he had rejected Christ for such temporal reasons, and that consequently he may never experience the saving power of Christ and the presence of God. It struck me that many people know Christ as Savior yet have never made Him Lord. **Many of the things that kept my friend from giving his life to Christ for salvation are the same things that keep many Christians from making Him Lord.** Romans 12:2 tells how conforming to the world blocks God's transformation:

> *Do not conform any longer to the pattern of this world, but be transformed by the renewing of your mind. Then you will be able to test and approve what God's will is — His good, pleasing and perfect will. (NIV)*

Culture is a powerful influencer that can quickly become your idol. You slowly substitute the culture's thinking, ways, beliefs, and habits for God's perfect ways. The culture comes to mean more than Christ Himself. 1 John 2:15 warns how this pushes God out of your life: *Do not love the world or anything in the world. If anyone loves the world, the love of the Father is not in him. (NIV)* Conforming to the culture is a normal way of life before most people know Christ as Savior; as a result it had come to feel right. Their former lifestyle masks the sin that is replacing their God.

The lifestyle and character of Christians will be what the world uses to describe a Christian. In the same way, a Christian's inconsistencies in lifestyle will be used by the world to define them as hypocrites. I was in a Bible study with a fellow Christian who avidly professed and followed Christ. Time and time again I heard stories about his language, the way he treated people, and some instances of dishonesty. Those who experienced his inconsistencies often commented, "If that is a Christian, I want nothing to do with Christianity."

Your actions are a product of your Lordship, but your Lordship follows your faith. Faith and Lordship feed on each other. God calls you to be filled with the Spirit instead of the world. It is out of the Spirit's filling that your faith is strengthened. In the same way, your Lordship grows as your faith grows, and your faith grows even more as you make Jesus Lord over more of your life. Obeying God out of Lordship even when you lack faith allows God to actively work in your life. Your Lordship allows God to strengthen your faith by working in your life. In Joshua 24:14, Joshua recognized this and challenged his people,

> *'Now fear the LORD and serve Him with all faithfulness. Throw away the gods your forefathers worshiped beyond the River and in Egypt, and serve the LORD.' (NIV)*

Joshua saw the corruption and sin that had enveloped his people. He knew that faith and Lordship go hand-in-hand. You cannot profess faith and follow the idols of this world. Faith poses the question of Lordship, "Do you believe Me enough to obey?" Believing God's ways and commands calls you to act on those beliefs by serving

Him. In Joshua 24:15b, Joshua called the peoples' faith to action, *'Then choose for yourselves this day whom you will serve.'* (NIV) Acting on your beliefs allows God to be Lord of your life. Do not forget that your beliefs flow out of the intimacy of your relationship in Christ.

☦

Ask yourself, "Where am I?" "Where have I conformed to the world and not made Jesus my Lord?"

POSITION 9 – HARD HEART

Proverbs 28:14 warns us about having a hard heart: *Blessed is the man who always fears the LORD, but he who hardens his heart falls into trouble.* (NIV) The one thing a Christian should not have is a hard heart. Christians often do have hard spots in their heart, and at times, hard hearts in general. Here are some examples of hard hearts:

- Being bitter and refusing to forgive and reconcile with others diminishes the unconditional love God extends to you. You should be able to forgive another if God was able to forgive you when you were dead in your sins.
- Allowing the way Christians act to affect your walk with Christ means you are making them, not Christ, your God.
- Allowing Christian organizations to drive you away from opportunities to grow and fellowship means you are placing your faith in institutions, not God.
- Being embittered to God due to a loss or difficult experience means you are not placing your hope in God, but in the things of this world.

A hard heart is usually reflective of many issues that are unrelated to why a person has hardened his or her heart. Ultimately, it reflects an attitude of unbelief in God. You can confront your difficulty with a hard heart by yourself or you can allow God to walk with you through the difficulty. Handling difficult life events in the way of the world requires you to harden your heart against God's ways. God wants difficulty to be an opportunity for Him to work in your life. Jesus says in Matthew 11:28-30,

'Come to Me, all you who are weary and burdened, and I will give you rest. Take My yoke upon you and learn from Me, for I am gentle and humble in heart, and you will find rest for your souls. For My yoke is easy and My burden is light.' (NIV)

A hardened heart becomes increasingly resistant and disconnected from the influence of the Holy Spirit. It moves progressively towards disobedience rather than obeying God. A Christian with a hard heart allows sin into his life and makes himself vulnerable to other sins. A hardened heart does what it wants, not what God wants, which ultimately puts sin on the throne of his life. Zechariah 7:12-13 shows God's response to one who lives with a hardened heart,

They made their hearts as hard as flint and would not listen to the law or to the words that the LORD Almighty had sent by His Spirit through the earlier prophets. So the LORD Almighty was very angry. 'When I called, they did not listen; so when they called, I would not listen,' says the LORD Almighty. (NIV)

The saddest thing about a hard heart is that it breaks your fellowship with God. Just as you cannot flourish in friendship with someone you are fighting with, you cannot grow in intimacy and fellowship with God when you have stuck your finger in His eye.

✞

Ask yourself, "Where am I?" "Do I have a hard heart towards any person, organization, or against God Himself?"

POSITION 10 – COMMITTED HEART

We have reviewed nine positions that reveal your relationship with God to God. You can perform all nine of these, but still lack commitment. 2 Chronicles 16:9a describes the type of person God wants to pour His life into: *For the eyes of the LORD range throughout the earth to strengthen those whose hearts are fully committed to Him. (NIV)* God wants you to have a heart that is fully committed to Him. You can live righteously, but without commitment you can quickly become misdirected. You can make Jesus "Lord," but without commitment to Him, you may not follow through. You can pursue proper use of the gifts and talents God has given you, but a lack of commitment can cause you to fall short. Many people begin with good intentions but fizzle out. **God wants to pour His life into those who do not just talk about Him, but those who are impassioned by the Holy Spirit to be committed and obedient to Him.**

A committed heart shows a change of ownership from things of this earth to the God of the universe. Philippians 3:20-21 explains the result of a change of ownership:

> *For our citizenship is in heaven, from which also we eagerly wait for a Savior, the Lord Jesus Christ; who will transform*

the body of our humble state into conformity with the body of His glory, by the exertion of the power that He has even to subject all things to Himself. (NASB)

A committed heart ties together who you are in Christ while helping you actualize all nine previouslydiscussed positions. A committed heart also reveals your pliability to be led and used by God. Proverbs 21:1 demonstrates this kind of heart: *The king's heart is like channels of water in the hand of the LORD; He turns it wherever He wishes. (NASB)* Christians who align well with God often fail because they lack pliability. Responding to Lordship at times seems easy, but as Lordship requires cost and demands change, do you have the pliability and commitment for God to continue? **Commitment pushes through the hardships of discipleship so that God can fully accomplish His purpose.**

☦

Ask yourself, "Where am I?" "What is my commitment to God? Do I have the tenacity to see it through?"

POSITION 11 – A SATISFIED HEART

The previous ten positions help evaluate where your heart is in its various facets. God wants to be in tune with you in every facet of your heart. Think of your heart as a prism that radiantly displays God's light through you, with each facet displaying Him in a different way. The more facets of your heart that radiate God's light, the more your heart is growing in satisfaction. David describes such a heart beautifully in Psalm 63:3-5:

Because Your love is better than life, my lips will glorify You. I will praise You as long as I live, and in Your name I will lift up my hands. My soul will be satisfied as with the richest of foods; with singing lips my mouth will praise You. (NIV)

God can accomplish great things through a heart that is aligned with Him. The presence and work of God occurs more freely when your heart is satisfied. Look at the ways David's heart expressed satisfaction in this passage:

- David followed and obeyed God not because he had to, but because he loved God more than anything else in this world.
- David saw no difference between word and action. God's truth automatically moved his heart to action. True obedience to God flows out of love, not duty.
- David saw advantages to both failure and success. Both were good because his hope was in God. He knew God would use both failure and success for His glory. David could praise God because He was in control. God was the source for David's life.
- David had learned that no temporal thing in this world could satisfy like God. God was the true satisfaction of David's heart.
- The satisfaction from God that David had in his heart reflected his relationship with God. God's life and presence in David radiated to those around him.

A satisfied heart is a heart that is consumed with Jesus. Nothing satisfies more.

✞

Ask yourself, "Where am I?" "Do I have a satisfied heart in God that takes whatever life dishes out?"

Where are you in Christ? Your position in Christ will determine Christ's life in you. Galatians 4:1 describes an impoverished life: *What I am saying is that as long as the heir is a child, he is no different from a slave, although he owns the whole estate.* (NIV) As a follower of Christ, you own the whole estate. All God's promises are yours. You are meant to not only have God's blessings, but to also do greater things than Jesus. Step back and size up who you are in Jesus. **Act on those areas where you fall short, so that you can grow to maturity and take hold of all God has for you.**

THREE

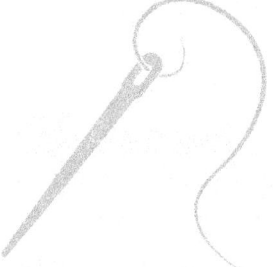

Making Your God Bigger

CHRISTIANS CAN INADVERTENTLY OR INTENTIONALLY make their God small. Whatever causes your God to become smaller ultimately begins to cripple your Christian walk. In Matthew 8:26 Jesus rebukes the disciples for believing so little in God's power, '*You of little faith, why are you so afraid?' Then He got up and rebuked the winds and the waves, and it was completely calm.* (NIV) Once you start believing your God is small, you miss many opportunities God has given you for growth, direction, and sanctification. The smaller your God becomes, the less you pray, mainly because you do not really believe God can answer your prayers. You pray halfheartedly for something because you do not believe it will happen. Your faith to trust God with a difficulty becomes less because you do not believe He is in control. Your mouth says you believe, but your heart and actions say you do not. Making God small causes your walk with Him to become void of pursuit, zeal, and conviction. The teachings and promises you hear are good, but not good enough to believe with conviction.

Ezekiel 33:31 gives a description of what could be a group of Christians who make their God smaller by making the things of this world their god:

> *My people come to You, as they usually do, and sit before You to listen to Your words, but they do not put them into practice. With their mouths they express devotion, but their hearts are greedy for unjust gain. (NIV)*

A heart that is greedy for unjust gain diminishes God by seeking the creation rather than the Creator. Such a hearts seek what they want instead of what God wants. They put their desires before God's desires. The lives they live are not for God, but for themselves. Breaking God's laws for personal gain has become not just acceptable, but commonplace. Compromising for political correctness or safely living the Christian life so that no one will be offended not only diminishes God, but also begins to exclude Him from being the God of your life. Living life in these ways makes life about you instead of glorifying God. You make your God smaller when you do not think He needs to be involved. You are missing God's best any time you make Him too small to meet your needs. The way you embrace God's promises and truths ultimately reflects the size of your God. **You will experience more of the living God the larger you allow your God to be.**

You live in a world that can quickly desensitize you to God. You have learned to believe what you see, get what you desire, and hear what you want. Matters are made worse by the expectation of getting what you want instantly. Why wait for God when you can get what you want now? Is your God big enough to trust, follow, suffer for, and sacrifice for, or is He just big enough to give an hour on Sunday and a little of your excess time throughout the week? Is your God big enough to be a part of all the areas of your life? **As your God grows in your heart and mind, so will your faith — a faith that chooses Him over the tangible things of this world.**

The size of your God is ultimately determined by the love you have for Him in your heart. Luke 6:45 gives a glimpse of this:

> *The good man brings good things out of the good stored up in his heart, and the evil man brings evil things out of the evil stored up in his heart. For out of the overflow of his heart his mouth speaks. (NIV)*

How badly do you want your God to be bigger? How committed are you to making necessary changes in areas of your life where you have pushed God out? Are you desperate enough to make God as big in your life as He truly is? Could you say, as David did in Psalm 63:1: . . .*My soul thirsts for You, my body longs for You, in a dry and weary land where there is no water.* (NIV) Let God use the following nine indicators for allowing God to be as big as He really is. Each of these areas will draw you deeper into a living, personal relationship with Jesus allowing your God to become bigger.

OUR INCOMPARABLE, INCOMPREHENSIBLE, WONDERFUL GOD

The beginning of making your God bigger is to grasp just how big your God is. The shear attributes and character of God are overwhelming, yet we often relate to the magnificence of God's attributes and character with a long, drawn-out yawn. We try to capture who God is by describing Him as omniscient, omnipotent, and omnipresent. These are stuffy words that do describe who God is, but somehow, they do not capture how incomparable and wonderful He is compared to anything you can imagine or have. These three descriptions do not begin to touch God's incomprehensible personality and character.

Both the nature of who God is and His character are integral to how big your God is in your life. Psalm 36:5-9 beautifully captures some of God's nature and character:

Your love, O LORD, reaches to the heavens, Your faithfulness to the skies. Your righteousness is like the mighty mountains, Your justice like the great deep. O LORD, You preserve both man and beast. How priceless is Your unfailing love! Both high and low among men find refuge in the shadow of Your wings. They feast on the abundance of Your house; You give them drink from Your river of delights. For with You is the fountain of life; in Your light we see light. (NIV)

Failing to capture the fullness of who God is makes Him smaller and makes it more difficult to grasp who He is. This passage combines many of God's creations with His character: heaven with His love; the scope of His righteousness with the magnificence of the earth's many mountain ranges; His justice with the indescribable depths found in many of the earth's bodies of water; and His protection, comfort and security in the shadow of His wings. Combining His loving nature with His awe-inspiring creation is breathtaking. This passage gives power to God's omnipotence by combining them with the character traits that feed the human spirit. Can you imagine embracing God by faith without experiencing His love, compassion, justice, righteousness, security, grace, and mercy?

Each step of faith exposes you to more of God — a God who is more wonderful and faithful than you can ever imagine. Your steps of faith reveal a little more of God each time which will strengthen your faith. This relationship between faith and understanding your God is a major factor in making your God bigger. The following description of God is not complete, but it is a personalized paraphrase to help you comprehend who is your heavenly Father. Listen to the Holy Spirit in you to recognize that your God is big enough to not only handle your issues, but also the issues throughout the earth.

This description comes from over 20 verses. Each description is referenced by the verse from which it came:

As I gaze at the beauty of the clouds, I am awed at the mastery of my God. When I am jolted and frightened by the flashes of lightening, I see them in perspective of an all-powerful, majestic God (Job 37:15). I can come to my Father because He knows me (Psalm 139:1). I am anxious to talk to God each morning, because He loves me for who I am and just the way I am. I do not have to hide anything from You because while I was sinful and undeserving, Jesus Christ died for me. You accepted and forgave me just as I was. (Romans 5:8) Even when I fail again, Your love is constant and enduring forever – even to 1,000 generations (Deuteronomy 7:9). I can bring to You any of my problems from small to large and You understand them all. You perceive my thoughts before I even come to You (Psalm 139:2). I do not have to explain my ways because You know the most intimate details of my life (Psalm 139:3). When the world is closing in around me and all my problems are suffocating me, You surround me with Your love and covering while holding and guiding me (Psalm 139:5). When sin has consumed me and I am driven to desperation, You are there. Wherever I go, You are with me with arms open wide. Wherever You take me in life, whether wealthy or poor, successful or a failure, You are there for me

(Psalm 139:7-10). No one knows me better than You. You created me, knitting together my every part in my mother's womb. There is no part of my creation that You did not have Your hand on (Psalm 139:13-15). I am comforted because all the days ordained for me were written in Your book before one of them came to be. Nothing is going to happen to me that is not already known and ordained by You (Psalm 139:16). I know Your ways are just. I am Your perfect work. I stand on You, my perfect Rock, who is faithful and will do me no wrong. You are just in all you do (Deuteronomy 32:4). You have no evil in You. (Job 34:10). You live forever in a Holy place. I desire that holiness. I am so thankful I will be with You eternally. You ask nothing of me but to have a contrite and humble spirit that will submit to You, so that You can always revive me (Isaiah 57:15). Your ways are rock-solid, joyful, and filled with life. No matter the circumstances, Your ways are true and everlasting (Psalm 119:142). Unlike man You are true to Your Word. When You speak, You act; when You promise, You fulfill (Numbers 23:19). I feel Your love and compassion and am humbled by Your gracious love (Psalm 116:5). I am humbled that You have kept Your promises. Your perseverance and patience show Your great love for all who come to You in salvation (2 Peter 3:9). You are so good (2 Chronicles 5:13) and loving (1 John 4:8). You fill the earth with Your presence and love (Jeremiah 23:24). I am so grateful You do not change (Malachi 3:6). I can trust and follow You because You are the same yesterday, today, and forever (Hebrews 13:8).

In Job 37:14 Elihu tells Job, 'Listen to this, Job; stop and consider God's wonders.' (NIV)

Yes, God is big enough to trust, follow, suffer for, and wait on.

TAKE YOUR POSITION

Every Christian has a belief system about God. A person's belief system should adhere to God's promises and truths in His Word. The belief system a person has is ultimately revealed by how he follows and obeys God's promises and truths. Psalm 147:10-11 explains how your belief system should be one of trust in your Lord: *His pleasure is not in the strength of the horse, nor His delight in the legs of a man. The LORD delights in those who fear Him, who put their hope in His unfailing love.* (NIV) God's pleasure is not in what you do for Him, but in the position you take in trusting Him. You can take one of four positions as a Christian.

1. You have made Jesus Lord of your life, so that everything in your life flows from Him.
2. You are your own Lord and everything that happens in your life will come from your talents, ingenuity, and perseverance.
3. Relationships, technology, knowledge, and the tools of this world will get you whatever you want.
4. A combination of the previous three.

The underlying belief of Positions Two and Three is that your God is not enough to handle what life dishes out.

Early in my Christian walk, I was voraciously reading, studying, and memorizing the Word. God was all over my life. I was consumed with God. One autumn I took a trip with some fellow counselors from a Christian camp I worked at during the summer. We were to spend three days in Colorado. On the first day, I took off for a hike. My objective was the mountaintop. Going up was easy. I knew the way by the mountain peak that was always in sight. Coming down was a different story. I quickly became disoriented. No path I took was taking me back to my camp. My adventure turned into being lost and ill-prepared for a night in the mountains. By the dawn of morning I had run into a bear, learned that fires are not easily lit without matches, and realized that the mountains get very cold at night. I would have preferred being back at camp eating a juicy steak, as was planned. All throughout this ordeal Psalm 75:6-7, which I had recently memorized, kept going through my head:

> *No one from the east or the west or from the desert can exalt a man. But it is God who judges: He brings one down, He exalts another. (NIV)*

Throughout the night, I calculated how to get down the mountain. Simultaneously, Psalm 75:6-7 kept going through my mind. By morning, my plan was to try the path I had mentally reconstructed during the night to find my way back. If that did not work, I would go back to the mountain stream I had crossed and follow it to a town I had seen in the distance. I prayed, entrusting my predicament to God. Very quickly, I came to a clearing that had a search plane with forest rangers gearing up to search for me.

Humility in hand, a hungry stomach, and with Psalm 75:6-7 fresh on my mind, I heard a clear message from God. **My position is to let God take me through life. No amount of Scripture memory and Bible study can ever replace God. Only God is going to take me into His plans.** I quickly saw how my zeal for God had pushed Him out of the driver's seat and me into it. What a rich lesson for a young Christian who really sought God's will and ways. Even with the pureness of my heart to do the right thing, I had pushed God aside and taken over. **God alone will take you into His purpose. If you want God's best, you must stand down and let God stand up.**

What is your position in Christ? Is God in control, or everything else but God? When you become smaller, your God becomes bigger. Your flesh always wants things we can see and touch to be in charge of, but God wants your love that is expressed through faith. Know that God alone can usher you into a better relationship with Him. It is God who will expand the horizon of His love for you. Growing in relationship and cultivating a deeper love for God will make it easier for you to trust Him. Trusting God is the actualization of your faith. As you live by an increasing measure of faith you will see your God grow in size. Psalm 37:5 says: *Commit your way to the LORD; trust in Him, and He will act. (RSV)*

FEARING GOD

Psalm 147:11 points to what brings God delight: *The LORD delights in those who fear Him, who put their hope in His unfailing love. (NIV)* Fearing God used to make me feel uncomfortable. It just did not seem to fit with the God who loved me so much that He sacrificed His Son for my sins. Why would I fear someone who loved me so much that He would die for me? As I grew in my relationship with Christ, it became clear that this fear was not in terror of Him, but in awe and reverence of Him.

Your fear of God is closely tied to your intimacy with Christ. The greater your relationship with Christ, the greater your wonder and fear of Him. Your wonder will not only lead you to know God better, but it will also allow you to approach life with a new appreciation for the grace God has poured into your life. Your view of God will enlarge like a balloon as you grow in the intimacy of your relationship with Christ and your wonder of who He is. As your realization of God grows, you will begin to take greater steps of obedience. Your obedience will further enlarge your faith. A growing faith will expose you to more of God's hand at work, which further magnifies the size and understanding of your God.

A deepening relationship with God changes how you relate to

God. God's life in you will move your faith from seeking intellectual understanding to visually seeing who God is from your life experiences with Him. This knowledge and understanding of God will show how your earthly desires and efforts fall short of Him, and help you understand why others will always fail you compared to the faithfulness of God. You and others may fall short, but your God never will. It is out of this ever-enlarging wonder of God that you can truly fear Him. A fear not out of terror, but a fear out of awe of who He is!

This life of relationship with God, fear/wonderment, and faith will constantly confront the realities of your flesh. Our human response is to take control while excluding God. This response reflects pride by turning to self instead of God. Dealing with your internal and external struggles with sin in this way will only suck the life out of God's work in you. Psalm 10:4 describes this well: *In his pride the wicked does not seek Him; in all his thoughts there is no room for God.* (NIV)

It is during the times when your flesh rules that your wonderment of God turns to fear, because you see your hand, not God's, at work. As I have matured in my walk with Christ, these times become less frequent and my repentance comes quicker. I hasten to be absorbed into God's loving arms and the work of grace through the Holy Spirit in me. **My desire and longing for God's unfettered presence causes me to stand down so that God can fully stand up in my life.** You begin to better understand the fear of God when you fear any slipping away or squelching of His presence. Your fear is not of God, but of the potential of any breach in His precious presence and love in your life. You are assured by John 10:28 that though you live in an imperfect body, you live by the power of a perfect and loving God who loves you so much that He gave His Son for your sins and eternal protection. Jesus promises, '*I give them eternal life, and they shall never perish; no one can snatch them out of My hand."* (NIV)

KNOWING GOD'S LOVE

Everything in your Christian life will flow out of your relationship with Christ. It is out of the depth of your relationship with Christ that you will know God's love. Psalm 103:11-13 describes the vastness of God's love:

For as high as the heavens are above the earth, so great is His love for those who fear Him; as far as the east is from the west, so far has He removed our transgressions from us. As a father has compassion on his children, so the LORD has compassion on those who fear Him. (NIV)

Knowing God's love is talked about so much that it is often taken for granted. Yet when God's love is compared to how high are the heavens above the earth, it is nothing normal! The other day I asked my four-year-old grandson "How much does Poppy love you?" We entered a contest of describing our love for one another. I raised my hand, then jumped, touching the wall. I then pointed to the ceiling. We went outside and pointed to the clouds. By this time, we were profusely laughing. But I could have taken out my binoculars and stretched his imagination even more, or even gone to the science museum and used an enormous telescope. With each of these actions, my expressed love would grow with my grandson. This is similar to God. With each step of faith, you experience more of God and consequently more of His love. As demonstrated by my story, God's love is unending. The better news is that God desires to engulf your life with His love.

In Romans 8:15, Paul took God's love for you to a new level by making you His child and He your Father:

For you did not receive a spirit that makes you a slave again to fear, but you received the Spirit of sonship. And by Him we cry, 'Abba, Father.' (NIV)

I recently had dinner with a friend who adopted a child from his (now) ex-wife's previous marriage. He shared some of the things he still did for his adult child. Even though his child was not from him, he took on full legal and parental responsibilities when he adopted her. He is now divorced from her mother, but she is still his child. Yes, she is now an adult, but she is still his child. In Romans 8:38-39, God replicates the human act of adoption by promising not to abandon or disown you. You are His child who was adopted at salvation.

For I am convinced that neither death nor life, neither angels nor demons, neither the present nor the future, nor any powers, neither height nor depth, nor anything else in all creation, will be able to separate us from the love of God that is in Christ Jesus our Lord. (NIV)

The difference between claiming your position in Christ or disowning it is the difference between a victorious Christian life or being swallowed up by this world. 1 Peter 2:10 describes your position in Christ:

Once you were not a people, but now you are the people of God; once you had not received mercy, but now you have received mercy. (NIV)

God loves you and wants you to live as His child. Living this way allows you to live life with God, who can easily devour whatever the world dishes out. This is the same God who filled Paul and Silas with the joy to sing while in prison, who also filled Paul with praise for God when he was flogged, and who filled Peter with more care about the prison guard than his freedom when he had the opportunity to escape jail. God's love can take your bleakest moments and fill them with hope, perspective, peace, and joy. Jesus answered the disciples' response "That is impossible," in Mark 10:27 by saying, *With man this is impossible, but not with God; all things are possible with God.* (NIV) As you fall more in love with Jesus, the size of your God will grow in your life. Allow your God to become big enough to change your black-and-white picture to one that radiates the beauty and color that God desires for you!

DIE TO SELF

Many Christians who are flat in their faith, growth, and experience with God wonder why their relationship with Christ does not match His promise for the purpose and abundance in John 10:10: . . .'*I came that they may have life, and have it abundantly.*' (NRSV) The answer to this question often lies in how you relate to God on a daily basis. Does God have any effect on your life? How would your life change if God were no longer a part of it?

A Christian's growth with God is often stunted when their eyes are on the temporal instead of the eternal. The wife of a man whom I was discipling was struggling with the desire to work fewer hours so that she could be more involved with her children's upbringing. During this process, her husband was forced to take a new job that paid less. This change caused them to shelve their plans for her to work less. Upon asking why, he responded that their income had been drastically cut. I said, "Your income (a circumstance of life) does not determine your decision, but what God wants determines your decision." Worse yet was that their combined income would still be well over six figures. They were already living a modest lifestyle, so this change could easily be accomplished through minor adjustments. The barrier was not their inability, but their unwillingness to adjust their lives for what God wanted.

In Luke 21:4 you see the contrast of following God according to the sufficiency of your temporal wealth verses the sufficiency of God. Jesus taught, *'All these people gave their gifts out of their wealth; but she out of her poverty put in all she had to live on.'* (NIV) Her decision to give was not made out of her ability to do so, but out of God's leading in her life. God's work and purpose will continually be challenged by the things of this world. Your faith can be undercut by temporal desires that come before God. Your desires for the things of this world can be so strong that your fear of losing them is greater than your desire for God. Colossians 3:1-3 describes the solution to this predicament:

Since then, you have been raised with Christ, set your hearts on things above, where Christ is seated at the right hand of God. Set your minds on things above, not on earthly things. For you died, and your life is now hidden with Christ in God. (NIV)

Keep your eyes on Jesus and His eternal purpose. Determining your walk and life in Christ according to your ability can quickly undermine God's work. Trust God's faithfulness as you move forward in His will.

Your fear of losing the temporal can be overcome when your heart, mind, and spirit are captivated by God. God's ways will become your desires, resulting in a larger God. A larger God will more easily consume your fears, helping you to let go of the things of this world. As you keep seeking the things above and not the things of this earth, your heart will be captured by an irrational exuberance for God. Every step of faith will be met with the excitement of the opportunity of seeing God's hand at work. Mark 10:32 shows how fear can be replaced with the astonishment of what God is about to do:

They were on their way up to Jerusalem, with Jesus leading the way, and the disciples were astonished, while those who followed were afraid. (NIV)

Those followers of Jesus whose faith in God was growing lived in the expectation of seeing God work. Those who feared for themselves while following kept God (Jesus) at a safe distance. This describes so many Christians. Christians want more of Christ but are unwilling to let go of the things of the world. Until you are willing to let go, be vulnerable, and trust God, your God will be small in your life. But when you look to heaven, place your trust in God, die to self, and walk with Him, you will enter the realm of God where He is allowed to thrive in you.

ABSOLUTE TRUST

Faith is at the heart of every action you take when you make God bigger in your life. Your faith in God is at the root of *every* decision you make. Learning to trust God allows Him to be God in your life. Every time you trust God, your faith muscle grows. Daniel 3:16-18 offers a wonderful example of rebuking this world with absolute trust in God:

Shadrach, Meshach and Abednego replied to the king, 'O Nebuchadnezzar, we do not need to defend ourselves before you in this matter. If we are thrown into the blazing furnace, the God we serve is able to save us from it, and He will rescue us from your hand, O king. But even if He does not, we want you to know, O king, we will not serve your gods or worship the image of gold you have set up.' (NIV)

You can discern from their answer that this was not the first time they had trusted God. Their boldness and confidence showed they did not have a casual, on-call relationship with God, but a passionate, living relationship that allowed them to truly know their God. Their absolute trust in God pointed to a seasoned faith that had been tested many times before.

Their God was bigger than the king. *The size of their God was not reliant on outcomes, but on the firm foundation of who they knew Him to be.* Jesus describes this foundation of God that you can trust in Matthew 7:24-27,

'Therefore everyone who hears these words of Mine and puts them into practice is like a wise man who built his house on the rock. The rain came down, the streams rose, and the winds blew and beat against that house; yet it did not fall, because it had its foundation on the rock. But everyone who hears these words of Mine and does not put them into practice is like a foolish man who built his house on sand. The rain came down, the streams rose, and the winds blew and beat against that house, and it fell with a great crash.' (NIV)

You can have a foundation built on Jesus Christ, your rock, or you can build your foundation on sand. Basing your life on Jesus builds on rock, but establishing your foundation on the ways of the world builds on sand. Every decision is one of trusting God or trusting the ways of the world. Every time you trust God, your God grows a little more in your life. Not that God changes, but that your knowledge and experience with God grows where you are able to lay another faith paver in the foundation of your life. In Daniel 3:28, you see the results of trusting God regardless of the outcome:

> *Then Nebuchadnezzar said, 'Praise be to the God of Shadrach, Meshach and Abednego, who has sent His angel and rescued His servants! They trusted in Him and defied the king's command and were willing to give up their lives rather than serve or worship any god except their own God.' (NIV)*

They trusted God even if it meant death, because either way they were in God's hands. You see how something much better resulted, because they trusted God, not their temporal desires. They not only survived the fire, but Nebuchadnezzar came to know God!

Our God is often small in our lives because we think small and on a temporal level. Shadrach, Meshach, and Abednego could have focused only on staying alive, but instead they trusted God. They had no way of knowing how King Nebuchadnezzar would be affected, but God knew what could and would happen! Learning to trust God leads to a bigger God in your life. Are you willing to make your God bigger so that He can touch the lives of those around you?

OWNED BY GOD

Most of you reading this book have worked for an employer. When you go to work for someone else, you submit yourself to their authority. You do not have the right to dictate your job description. You only have the right to work — or not work — for your employer. If you choose to perform outside your job description, you move away from the direction of your employer. Your employer will now be forced to work with you to get you to perform within your job description. If you continue to perform poorly, your employer will begin disciplinary correction to bring you into alignment with his wishes. The same is true spiritually. Psalm 73:26 is a spiritual mirror of a secular employer:

Whom have I in heaven but You? And earth has nothing I desire besides You. My flesh and my heart may fail, but God is the strength of my heart and my portion forever. (NIV)

This passage beautifully describes a person who has turned over the ownership of his life to his Lord. Becoming a Christian involves two distinct processes: faith and Lordship. Making Jesus Lord of your life is turning over the ownership of your life to Him. You no longer live your life for your pleasure, but for God' pleasure and delight. Choosing things outside of God's desires makes your God smaller in your life. Not only does your God become smaller, but you also diminish how He is working in your life. God's focus moves from purpose to correction. God cannot use your Godly character to affect others' lives if you are not reflecting Godly character. God must first bring about Godly character so that you can be as 2 Corinthians 2:15 proclaims: *For we are to God the aroma of Christ among those who are being saved and those who are perishing. (NIV)* **Choosing your ways instead of God's way causes you to settle for less than God desires for you.**

Your life was self-centered before Christ. You lived primarily for yourself. Learning to live for God after receiving Christ takes some reprogramming. God has reprogrammed you by giving you a new heart. Yet, even with a new heart, your old self will continue to resist making Christ the Lord of your life. Rejecting God's leadings indicates God is insufficient for you, that what God offers is not big enough for your dreams and desires. The Old Testament calls idols those areas that you put before God. You worship and seek your idols more than God and have thus made them your god. Joshua 24:14 tells you to fear God and throw away those things you have made idols in your life,

'Now fear the LORD and serve Him with all faithfulness. Throw away the gods your forefathers worshiped beyond the River and in Egypt, and serve the LORD.' (NIV)

God desires your total devotion. God wants you to experience the fullness of His love by not wasting your life on the temporal things of this world. Philippians 3:18-19 shows the folly of worshipping the temporal instead of God:

For, as I have often told you before and now say again even with tears, many live as enemies of the cross of Christ. Their destiny is destruction, their god is their stomach, and their glory is in their shame. Their mind is on earthly things. (NIV)

Every human being needs nutrition to stay alive. You can chew on rubber, eat bark, and suck on steel bars, but none of them will take care of your physical requirements for food. Psalm 73:26 ends by telling you to make God your portion: *God is the strength of my heart and my portion forever. (NIV)* Only God can satisfy. Your priorities change once you make God your portion where He alone meets your needs. Your faith in God has grown to where God's ways and not the world's ways fully satisfy you. Ordering your life around God, and not idols that traditionally met your needs, will help you see and respond to God's direction. As your God grows in size, you will more easily trust Him with your priorities and activities because you have seen how He alone satisfies.

SEEKING AND WAITING ON GOD

We live in a society that does not wait and has little patience. We seek action and results immediately. Yet some of God's greatest work is done and discovered in prayer, waiting, and meditation.

Lamentations 3:24-26 shows the importance of waiting on and seeking God when you make Him your portion:

'The LORD is my portion,' says my soul, 'Therefore I have hope in Him.' The LORD is good to those who wait for Him, to the person who seeks Him. It is good that he waits silently for the salvation of the LORD. (NASB)

God will satisfy your desires and needs when He is your portion. The real question is whether you will have the patience to allow God to do it. **A wonderful admonition is to seek God's face and not His hand.** Focusing on the wonder and grace of God makes waiting on Him much easier. When your focus is on God's hand and what He will give you, your heart is erroneously set on getting from God instead of enjoying His love, presence, and His purpose for you. The inability to wait inadvertently says that God alone cannot provide or is not enough. Waiting on God with this belief is difficult because it says that not only is your relationship with Him shallow, but that your God is small. The greater your relationship with God the more satisfying His presence, and the easier it is to wait on Him. Live your Christian life so that God alone satisfies the needs of your life.

Waiting is not always passive. Waiting gives God the time to combine your desires with His desires. Lamentations 3:24-26 also said *to seek Him*. Waiting gives God room to ignite your desires for a kingdom purpose resulting in a passion to seek Him. Seeking is not praying five seconds while the phone is ringing, but **passionately seeking God's will because your hope is God**! You pray fervently, search the Bible with hunger, and enjoin fellow believers in your need. You approach God with a passion that says God alone can satisfy. He is your portion and salvation. This resolve says God is worth the wait.

The bigger your God, the firmer your hope will be. It is your hope in God that drives you to seek Him. You are willing to seek and wait on Him; because He alone understands you and can meet your needs in a way that the world cannot. Your hope is not desolate, because you know that your God is in control and quite capable of meeting your needs. It is this God that fills you with peace.

DELIGHT IN THE LORD

The final indicator of having a God who is big is your delight in Him. Psalm 37:4 shows the importance of finding delight in God: *Delight yourself in the LORD and He will give you the desires of your heart.* (NIV) Your delight in God shows a heart that beats to God's heart instead of a heart that beats to the drum roll of law (rules to live life by). Trusting, waiting, submitting, fearing, and seeking God can all be difficult, but remember your delight comes out of the intimacy of your relationship with God. Your God has grown bigger in your life because you know Him and love Him. You trust your God for big things because you have seen His work and delight in what He has done. You trust God's ways because you know He has your best interests at heart. You have seen what the world offers and delight in what God gives, because it is so much better.

A person who has been addicted to drugs or alcohol has an uphill battle in breaking their addictions. In fact, the relapse rate for addicts is over 80 percent. One of the reasons for this is the hole in their hearts. Reformed addicts are okay until the hole in their hearts yearn to be satisfied. This hole in the heart of an addict is often masked by a yearning for satisfaction by the things of this world. When those things do not satisfy, the ex-addict goes where they have always sought refuge in the past — their addiction. A similar principle is true for Christians who have replaced God in their lives with the substitutes of this world — recognition, friendships, self-worth, money, position, power … the list goes on. Until you delight in God alone, you will be lured by false idols that only bring temporary satisfaction, and eventually emptiness and destruction. God alone can satisfy your desires. Embracing the enormity of your God will allow Him to consume your false idols so that your true delight can come from Him.

Let your God become so big that your delight is in God's faithfulness. Only God alone is big enough to satisfy. The early disciples beautifully demonstrated their delight in Jesus in Acts 5:41: *The apostles left the Sanhedrin, rejoicing because they had been counted worthy of suffering disgrace for the Name* (Jesus). (NIV) Living your life in the delight of God's sufficiency visibly demonstrates your faith in how big your God is in your life.

Do not live your life in Christ like you are on a merry-go-round where you constantly want what is in front of you and behind you, but never getting it. Your God is big enough to bring true satisfaction. Use these nine indicators to help you recognize where you have made your God small, so that by faith you can fully embrace a God that is so much bigger than your desires and the things of this world. Allow these nine markers to fully enliven your heart to God, who He is, and what He desires for you.

FOUR

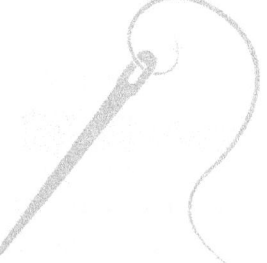

Positioning for the Eye of the Needle

EPHESIANS 4:22-24 PROVIDES A GOOD three-part outline for the rest of this book:

You were taught, with regard to your former way of life, to put off your old self, which is being corrupted by its deceitful desires; to be made new in the attitude of your minds; and to put on the new self, created to be like God in true righteousness and holiness. (NIV)

The first three chapters of this book were designed to help you see your life in terms of where you were and are in your relationship with Christ. It is difficult to grow, change, and experience more of Christ until you better understand where you are. Allowing the Holy Spirit to uncover opportunities for change in the first three chapters will show where your old self lives. Any place your old self lives ultimately pushes God aside. Understanding the old self prepares you to "put off the old" for you to "be made new in the attitude of your mind." Chapters 5 and 6 will help you to "be made new in the attitude of your mind." Chapters 7, 8, and 9 will help you "put on the new self."

Dealing with the sin patterns of your old nature can quickly become an exhausting human effort. God's grace, revealed through your salvation in Christ, relieved you of the burden of changing your old nature by way of the law. Living under the law is when you live your life according to rules without the redemptive work of Christ on the cross. The new way is to allow the Holy Spirit to transform your life as you submit yourself to Christ. The law's role is to inform you where you are and why things are happening. Knowing is not enough to live righteously, because your flesh is ill-equipped to fight sin. "Positioning for the Eye of the Needle" will help you take the next step after better seeing where you are, so that you can align your life for the work of the Holy Spirit.

Positioning yourself to go through the eye of the needle boils down to becoming less, in order that Jesus can become more. David displayed this wonderfully in 2 Samuel 6:21-22 when he said, *'I will celebrate before the LORD. I will become even more undignified than this, and I will be humiliated in my own eyes. . .'* (NIV) Whatever it took for David to be better positioned for God's use was never too much for him. His pride, his kingly position, and even his wife could not keep him from being positioned for God's best. In this chapter, we will cover nine areas where your position in life may hinder the work of the Holy Spirit: righteousness, spiritual disciplines, God your sustainer, waiting on God, sold out, like a child, humility, being last, and serving. These positions are prone to being puffed up with self, causing the work of the Holy Spirit to be thwarted. 2 Corinthians 4:11-12 describes how God wants you to position yourself in all nine areas:

For we who are alive are always being given over to death for Jesus' sake, so that His life may be revealed in our mortal body. So then, death is at work in us, but life is at work in you. (NIV)

These nine positions are important for going through the eye of the needle. It is never enough to just know about something; you must act in any area where you have room for growth or change. Proverbs 10:14 points to the wisdom of applying what you learn: *Wise men store up knowledge, but the mouth of a fool invites ruin. (NIV)* You store up knowledge by learning it and applying it to your life. Hearing the Word without application has no effect on your life. Unapplied truths ultimately set you up for failure. Do not continue in the old ways in which you lived. In John 16:7-9, 13-15 Jesus talks about the Holy Spirit convicting and guiding you towards application,

'But I tell you the truth: It is for your good that I am going away. Unless I go away, the Counselor will not come to you; but if I go, I will send Him to you. When He comes, <u>He will convict the world of guilt in regard to sin and righteousness and judgment</u>. But when He, the Spirit of truth, comes, <u>He will guide you</u> into all truth. He will not speak on His own; He will speak only what He hears, and He will <u>tell you what is yet to come</u>. He will bring glory to Me by taking from what is Mine and <u>making it known to you</u>. All that belongs to the Father is Mine. That is why I said the Spirit will take from what is Mine and make it known to you.' (NIV)

It is not enough to just know where you are missing God; you must allow the Holy Spirit to take hold of you and guide you in God's truths for transformation by putting off the old self. Allow God to penetrate deeply into your life on each of these nine positions. Receive these truths and store them up for application in your life. Allow them to grip and move you to do what God is calling you to do, just as David said in 2 Samuel 6:22, *'I will become even more undignified than this, and I will be humiliated in my own eyes.'* (NIV)

POSITIONING FOR RIGHTEOUSNESS

A common mistake Christians make is confusing righteousness through God's grace (His unmerited favor) at salvation with our need for righteousness in order for sanctification to occur. Sanctification is the process of becoming like Christ. We easily buy into our inability to live righteously in a broken world while being aloof to the need to pursue righteousness. Christians miss the significance of righteousness and its importance in experiencing Christ. Living this way results in a dysfunctional Christian life that reaps an unbalanced relationship with God. Instead of displaying the fruit of righteousness (God's attributes and actions being displayed), Christians live in a purposeless vacuum that allows many corrupted beliefs to develop. Christians desiring the goodness of God's hand end up with a feeling of failure and a broken relationship with God. They want to experience the steady hand of God directing their lives, but instead they live in doubt and with a diminished purpose. This lifestyle begins to raise questions in the minds of believers concerning forgiveness and the security of their relationship with God.

Understanding that grace is married to righteousness begins to resolve this disconnect between righteousness and grace. It is naïve to think that you can live contrary to God's way and still experience His righteousness and blessings. Unless you have God's grace, you cannot live in righteousness. Conversely, God's grace is muted without righteousness. Romans 7:15 illustrates a life lived by law without grace, *For what I want to do I do not do, but what I hate, I do.* (NIV) Romans 8:1-4 reveals how grace releases righteousness into your life:

> *Therefore, there is now no condemnation for those who are in Christ Jesus, because through Christ Jesus the law of the Spirit of life set me free from the law of sin and death. For what the law was powerless to do in that it was weakened by the sinful nature, God did by sending His own Son in the likeness of sinful man to be a sin offering. And so He condemned sin in sinful man, in order that the righteous requirements of the law might be fully met in us, <u>who do not live according to the sinful nature but according to the Spirit</u>. (NIV)*

The key to this passage is the last line. **To live in God's righteousness, you must live according to the Spirit. God is not going to allow you to sit it out while He is trying to produce His life through you. You must respond to your new nature and the leading of His Spirit. The Spirit lives in you and is making Himself known, but are you responsive and willing? This is where grace and righteousness can divorce or grow in greater harmony.** You know what God wants by the guidance of the Holy Spirit in you. You feel the Holy Spirit's leading, but you go another direction. This action numbs your conscience, conflicts your spirit, and contorts your heart. It is no longer the Apostle Paul, but you that utters the words of Romans 7:15, *For what I want to do I do not do, but what I hate I do.* (NIV) This is not a fun existence. It is often worse than a nonbeliever's experience. **Doing battle with God is not much fun… and you never win!**

God does not want you living at the low level of just humanly existing, but living abundantly above it. Living abundantly begins with your affirmation and commitment to righteousness. This may sound semantic and even legalistic, but it is not. This is much like a pilot flipping on the autopilot switch in a plane. The autopilot, God, begins flying the plane. Each movement of the autopilot requires the pilot, you, to relent control. Can you imagine if the pilot intervenes in each of the autopilot's movements? The pilot is in a constant battle for control, which leads to mistakes, and it takes much more effort to get where God wants you to go. **Similarly, when you affirm God's life in you and commit to His righteousness and Lordship, God begins to take you into righteousness!** In other words, you can fight it or go with it. **You should relent and let God take control. Desire His best!**

God wants you to live in righteousness, because He created you to have a greater satisfaction and peace that flows out of living righteously. **You do not have to be dragged through the mud of life to be motivated toward righteousness. Merely affirm your belief in God and let Him take control.** Psalm 85:13 shows the power of this life: *Righteousness goes before him and prepares the way for his steps.* (NIV) A Christian who lives in righteousness is constantly laying solid stepping stones of faith, while a life fighting righteousness is constantly throwing grenades before himself. One lives on solid ground in God's hands, while the other is dodging self-inflicted bullets and being rocked by grenades going off due to the way they live. **Righteousness is not static but goes before you to prepare the way. Instead of living with the consequences of not choosing God's way, you live in the results that righteousness produces.** (I repeat my earlier statement again so as not to confuse the two sides of righteousness: you are made righteous at salvation and live righteously through the process of sanctification.)

Jesus said in Matthew 6:33 that the key to righteous living is your assent to it, *'But seek first His kingdom and His righteousness, and all these things will be given to you as well.'* (NIV) When you seek God first, you are stepping into a life of righteousness. This allows you to put a face to righteousness: Jesus. Falling in love with righteousness is not that difficult because righteousness prepares the way for your steps to become permanent stepping stones of faith. **Each time you do this, your heart will beat in closer rhythm to the heartbeat of God.** In this way, you are constantly positioning yourself for greater measures of God's life and work in you.

POSITIONING WITH SPIRITUAL DISCIPLINES

There is no more important tool for positioning to go through the eye of the needle than spiritual disciplines. Spiritual disciplines are activities that make you available for being touched or used by God. Conversely there is no more controversial topic than spiritual disciplines. Those opposed say God does not require disciplines, because you have a new heart and the Holy Spirit living within you guides you. They say spiritual disciplines can be legalistic and can bring out our sinful nature. They also say spiritual disciplines can quickly replace your walk with God. All these statements may be true, yet I argue that spiritual disciplines are critical for spiritual growth. Can you imagine going to work for a company that provides no structure, boundaries, feedback on performance, communication on plans, or encouragement on how you are doing? It does not end well. Unfortunately, most Christians live their Christian lives in an unstructured environment without any inspired path for connecting with God.

Isaiah 32:16 gives a wonderful picture of what results when you live in the empowerment of the Holy Spirit: *Justice will dwell in the desert and righteousness live in the fertile field.* (NIV) God's Spirit can be poured out in many ways, but the most prevalent is making yourself available to Him so that the Holy Spirit can work in you. The spiritual disciplines you employ in your life put you on God's easel for transformation. The more you open yourself to God, the more you allow God to convict, teach, and lead you. A life lived with few or no spiritual disciplines usually results in a Christian walk that resembles a desert. You are connecting little with God, receiving little nourishment, oblivious to His work in your life, unaware of sin at work in you, blind to God's will, and consequently experiencing little of the abundance God has for you. The life with spiritual disciplines resembles a fertile field. You are doing a number of things to develop fertile soil in which God can work. The results of these activities are righteousness and a life that represents and magnifies Christ. Spiritual disciplines are valuable tools that God can use for making your life fertile for His life in you. Quiet time, Scripture memory, Bible study, fellowship groups, meditation, fasting, and attending church will all provide great avenues for God to speak to you. On the other hand, if your life is barren of any spiritual disciplines, it is like living in the desert. A life lived in the desert is vulnerable to sin and all the negative effects of sin. Seek from God the spiritual disciplines that can help open more of your life to a larger measure of God's life.

God uses any spiritual discipline to better connect with Him, but the daily quiet time has the greatest potential for intimacy and growth with God. There is very little in life that does not get better with regular, repeat performance. The same is true with your daily quiet time, as you spend time with God in Bible reading and prayer. This set-apart time with God provides an avenue for Him to daily speak into and be involved in every element of your life. Psalm 90:14 beautifully describes your goal in the quiet time: *Satisfy us in the morning with Your unfailing love, that we may sing for joy and be glad all our days. (NIV)* **The quiet time is a vital time to not only connect with God, but to also grow in increasing pleasure of knowing Him.** Having your quiet time first thing in the morning gives you the greatest opportunity to live on a full tank of God's grace, love, and direction each day. Your daily quiet time gives God the opportunity to satisfy you with His living presence, correct where you have gone off course, fill your heart with the wonderful things He did the day before, and direct your steps for the day while giving you the understanding of how to accomplish what He has set out for you. No Christian can afford to go into a day without God's full armor. Imagine with me a battalion of soldiers going into battle. Some are without clothes, some just have underwear, others have more clothing, some Kevlar, some have weapons, and some have full body armor. Throughout the day, soldiers continue to gear up as the battle rages. Who will be most effective in the battle? Without question, it's the fully-armored soldier. Who is most likely to be wounded? Those not prepared or equipped for battle. Ephesians 6:12-18 talks about the armor of God and what each piece does in a Christian's life:

Therefore put on the full armor of God, so that when the day of evil comes, you may be able to stand your ground, and after you have done everything to stand. Stand firm then, with the belt of truth buckled around your waist, with the breastplate of righteousness in place, and with your feet fitted with the readiness that comes from the gospel of peace. In addition to all this, take up the shield of faith, with which you can extinguish all the flaming arrows of the evil one. Take the helmet of salvation and the sword of the Spirit, which is the word of God. And pray in the Spirit on all occasions with all kinds of prayers and requests. With this in mind, be alert and always keep on praying for all the saints. (NIV)

Look at the armor you are putting on. You are reaffirming the truths of God. You are solidifying righteousness as the protector of your heart. You commit to peace in all your relationships and activities. Use faith in God as your shield in every spiritual battle. You do not live in fear throughout the day, because you know your eternity is secure with Christ. You deal with every activity using God's truths, promises, and wisdom through the Word of God. Put on the full armor of God first thing each morning. Boldly and proudly wear it.

Where you spend your time usually reflects what you love. In the same way, spiritual disciplines reflect your love for God. Pick the spiritual disciplines that help you hear, experience, and commune with God. **But heed this advice and do what needs to be done to connect you with God**. You do not want the accomplishment of your spiritual disciplines to be the objective, but rather the cultivation of your love for God and your relationship with Him. Allow your spiritual disciplines to help you more passionately seek Jesus so that you attain deeper times of intimacy and communion with Him. You want to get up each day not consumed with the duty of your quiet time and how long it takes, but as Psalm 27:8 says: *My heart says of You, 'Seek His face!' Your face, LORD, I will seek.* (NIV) **Your obsession is not with the spiritual discipline, but to be consumed with a growing desire for more of the living God.** Your spiritual disciplines should move beyond having to do something to wanting the pleasure of communing with God. Be passionate in your spiritual disciplines, so that you are positioned to experience every ounce of God's love, grace, work, and presence.

At the end of the book, Appendix 2 Application: Feet for Applying God's Word, provides more detailed information on spiritual disciplines. This information may be helpful in starting certain spiritual disciplines. It may also help you enhance certain spiritual disciplines you already have. The word feet is used for spiritual disciplines as a metaphor for activities that take you to God.

POSITIONING GOD AS MY SUSTAINER

If you quit your job tomorrow, your change of income will affect the way you live. Your last child leaving home will affect the way you live. Moving from a comfortable life in suburbia to a mission field in a third-world country will change the way you live. **Will removing**

God from your life have any effect other than giving you more time? What difference does God make in your life? Many people would honestly have to say, "little or none." I asked a group of 18 Christians the other night to describe how they had communed with God that day. While one person had read the Bible and prayed in a focused way, only three others had prayed while walking, showering, or driving. Would it be fair to say that something else besides Jesus was sustaining these Christians?

In John 4:34 Jesus describes how His life was sustained by God: *'My food,' said Jesus, 'is to do the will of Him who sent Me and to finish His work.'* (NIV) Food is the primary sustainer of life for all humans. Without food you die. Beyond food's physical sustenance is the opportunity that eating food provides for socializing, conducting business, deepening relationships, and passing the time. You can quickly visualize a devastated life from going without food, but can you visualize Jesus' life apart from doing God's will? God was the center of Jesus' life. Everything in Jesus' life gravitated out of God's will. Just as your liver filters blood through your body, your life should be filtered through God's will. **Anything that you do that does not filter through God's will deprives you of His life in that area.**

Making God's will your food positions you for experiencing more of Him. Words such as portion, hunger, and thirst are words in the Bible that vividly demonstrate this position. If God's will is your food, you will hunger for righteousness. In Psalm 81:10 God declares not only His sovereignty, but also His desire to pour His life into you, *'I am the LORD your God, who brought you up out of Egypt. Open wide your mouth and I will fill it.'* (NIV) God does not want you to consume the least amount of His will, or what is most convenient or costs you the least. **He wants you to hunger for His will in a way that makes you available for whatever He has for you.** If your portion is God, the trinkets of this world will be secondary. If you thirst for God's presence, your priorities will align to keep you constantly in His presence.

Making God your sustaining food changes the way you live life. As food is not negotiable in your life, neither will God's presence and life in you be negotiable. You will become adaptable to what God puts before you instead of resistant. You will be amenable to applying God's truths instead of inflexible. You will relish more opportunities to walk by faith instead of being indifferent to faith opportunities. Psalm 107:9 says you should be positioned to be satisfied by God: *For He satisfies the thirsty and fills the hungry with good things.* (NIV) Your life with God will be radically different because of your increasing experiences with Him as your Sustainer.

God wants to be your food and drink. He desires to sustain you. For this to happen you must do as Jesus teaches in John 6:27 and live for God alone,

> *'Do not work for food that spoils, but for food that endures to eternal life, which the Son of Man will give you. On Him God the Father has placed His seal of approval.'* (NIV)

Position your life for God by making Him alone your Sustainer. Root out those things in life that are trying to satisfy that which only God can satisfy. Replace them with God's food. Step back and recognize what God is already doing to sustain you; as a result, you will be encouraged, strengthened, and focused. Deepen your yearning for God as Psalm 84:2 describes through the spiritual disciplines He has given: *My soul yearns, even faints, for the courts of the LORD; my heart and my flesh cry out for the living God.* (NIV) The more you allow God to be your sustainer, the more your life will be absorbed into His. You will begin to see that things you thought were important are now secondary. You will begin moving into the position Jesus describes in John 12:25, *'The man who loves his life will lose it, while the man who hates his life in this world will keep it for eternal life.'* (NIV) Allowing God to be your Sustainer truly positions you for more of Christ.

POSITIONING BY WAITING ON GOD

Impatience quenches the Spirit. Learning to wait on God allows the character of the believer to blossom and the work of the Spirit to be fully released in him. Not waiting on God causes believers to miss much of what God has for them. Psalm 91:1-2, 4 unfolds five principles of waiting on God:

> *He who dwells in the shelter of the Most High will rest in the shadow of the Almighty. I will say of the LORD, 'He is my refuge and my fortress, my God, in whom I trust.' ... He will cover you with His feathers, and under His wings you will find refuge; His faithfulness will be your shield and rampart.* (NIV)

The first principle of waiting on God is dwelling in God. Dwelling in God is the beginning of waiting on God. Too often waiting on God happens apart from dwelling in God. As you dwell in God, He will equip and guide you to wait on Him. Waiting on God apart from dwelling in God will often lead to procrastination and shirking your responsibilities. A great way to dwell in God is by fasting. I learned early in my walk with Christ the importance and power of fasting. God used several types of fasting in my pursuit of Him. During one of my fasts, I realized that I was waiting on God, but not dwelling in Him. I would fast but use my new-found time from not eating as extra time to get other things done. I was devoting minimal time to seeking God, to following Scriptural principles He was giving me, and to meditating on His Word as well as the thoughts that flowed from His Word. My fasting looked great spiritually, but I was missing rich opportunities to hear God and experience His presence, work, and direction in my life.

Learning to wait on God and dwell in Him may be one of the more difficult disciplines of a Christian. Creating an intentional environment for waiting and dwelling helps tremendously. Using these four **S**'s - **s**implicity, **s**ilence, **s**olitude, and **s**urrender - will help you wait on and dwell in God:

- **S**implicity. You live in a time where gadgets that **s**implify your life are multiplying at an exponential rate. Unfortunately, many of the new gadgets seem to consume more time than they save. The natural progression of increased wealth is the acquisition of more things. Each thing you own now owns you and takes a piece of your time. The menu of things available to do in life is continually expanding. Social media, smartphones, sports, hobbies, exercise routines, social clubs, church activities, electronic games, entertainment venues, television, and contrived activities all consume a portion of a person's day. Each item takes a piece of your life. Achieving a level of **s**implicity allows you to unwind your life enough to allow in more of God. You will struggle to wait and dwell with God If your life is so consumed with the personal, the world, vocation, and activities. Learn to **s**implify your life, so that you have time to truly wait on and dwell in God.
- **S**ilence. To hear God, you need **S**ilence. Find a place of **s**ilence. I asked a minister I was discipling about his quiet time. He said the first thing he did upon arriving at work was close the door to his office and have his quiet time. I asked if he was ever interrupted. He laughed and said that the phone was constantly ringing and there was continual knocking on the door. **S**ilence is not easy, but each person

must find their place of silence. **Work to eliminate the volume of noise, in order that the volume of God's voice in your life can increase.**

- **S**olitude. Simplicity and silence are powerful in helping you to learn to wait on God and dwell in Him, but solitude is a state of being that can amplify or sabotage both. Solitude gives you an environment to persevere in waiting and multiplies the impact God has on your waiting and dwelling with Him. Learning to enter a state of solitude allows you to reduce, if not eliminate, the clutter in your mind. Our fast-paced world has sped up our mental processes to such a level that it becomes difficult to pray, meditate, wait on, and dwell in the Lord. Allow God's peace to consume the mind's clutter so that you can wait in solitude instead of the busy intersection of life's activities. Solitude helps bring clarity and peace while you wait on God and dwell in Him.
- **S**urrender. Many of the points in the previous chapters have helped you identify things in your life that need to be surrendered. Waiting on God's answer and direction is wonderful, but if you are not willing to surrender, you will be sabotaging God's work in you. Surrender removes the obstacles that are blocking God's message. Desire what God has for you more than the things to which you are clinging.

The four **S**'s will fuel your ability to wait and hear. **Waiting in the intimacy and love of Father God enlarges the wonder and expectation of God's work.** Conversely, your failure to wait usually points back to your lack of intimacy with God.

Learning to rest in God is the second principle that will help you wait on God. Jesus said this in Matthew 11:28, *'Come to Me, all you who are weary and burdened, and I will give you rest.'* (*NIV*) It is difficult to wait when your life is falling apart, but resting in God points to the transference of your burdens to God. Resting in God spares you the agony of what is happening to you while allowing you the comfort of God's love and care. Give your burdens to God and trust Him to bring about His perfect result!

Your ability to wait reflects the third principle of having faith in God's ability to act. The bigger your God becomes, the easier it will be to allow Him to be your refuge and fortress. Impatience reflects a lack of faith in God to handle what is happening. Your ability to trust God to care for you echoes a faith that says, "I believe my God is in control." Failing to wait on God shows an impatience that says "I can do it better than God."

The fourth principle of waiting on God is believing God is able to protect you. Failure to wait often comes from the fear of loss. Like a mother hen covering her chicks with her wings and feathers, your God is not only able to protect you, but also refresh you. Envision and feel God pulling you into His care while providing safety and comfort. It is this safe and comforting place that allows you to wait on God. How great is our God!

The fifth principle of waiting is that God wants to demonstrate His faithfulness. Experiencing God's faithfulness comes from walking with Him on a daily basis. Encountering God's faithfulness allows you to see God Himself expressing His faithfulness to be there for you and take care of you. Each time you wait, you allow God the opportunity to give you what He has for you and to allow Him to further sculpt the full character of Himself in you. Engage times of waiting by embracing the truth that God truly cares for you and will take care of you. Psalm 27:4 speaks to enjoying the wait (rest):

One thing I have asked from the LORD, that I shall seek: That I may dwell in the house of the LORD all the days of my life, to behold the beauty of the LORD, and to meditate in His temple. (NASB)

POSITIONING BY BEING SOLD OUT

Philippians 3:8-10 presents one of the most challenging positions for a Christian:

> *I count all things to be loss in view of the surpassing value of knowing Christ Jesus my Lord, for whom I have suffered the loss of all things, and count them but rubbish in order that I may gain Christ, and may be found in Him, not having a righteousness of my own derived from the Law, but that which is through faith in Christ, the righteousness which comes from God on the basis of faith, that I may know Him, and the power of His resurrection and the fellowship of His sufferings, being conformed to His death. (NASB)*

This passage gives three major mindsets that challenge a believer's core belief in God. These three mindsets are so contrary to the world's thought process that they demand you ask the question, "Are you sold out to Jesus?"

The first mindset of a Christian asks the question, "Are you ready to give up whatever is required to make Jesus number one in your life?" Loss of possessions, relationships, aspirations, vocation, and location are all on the table for making Jesus number one. 2 Corinthians 4:17 shows how being sold out to Jesus may involve loss, but your loss is far outweighed by the joy of following and experiencing Christ: *For our light and momentary troubles are achieving for us an eternal glory that far outweighs them all. (NIV)* This mindset allows a deepening and expanding relationship with Jesus, which makes the things of this world look like rubbish.

The second mindset is knowing and living your life out of your identity in Christ. We live in a performance-oriented world where doing equates to achieving. Doing and achieving can quickly give you authority and stature, but possibly at the cost of displacing Christ. Righteousness comes not from what you do but is given to you at salvation and manifests in your life as you live it out by faith in Christ. 2 Corinthians 11:30 proclaims your identity is in Christ — not in what you do: *If I must boast, I will boast of the things that show my weakness.* (NIV) Living through your identity in Christ frees you from the world's continual treadmill of performing and proving your identity.

The final mindset is seeing suffering as a natural byproduct of being conformed to the image of Christ and living according to His will. The laws of nature say that if it hurts, do not do it. Your faith walk with Christ is quite different. **Suffering as a Christian provides some of the best venues for allowing God to refine, teach, or use you in the life of another.** That's why Peter wrote in 1 Peter 1:7:

> *These have come so that your faith — of greater worth than gold, which perishes even though refined by fire — may be proved genuine and may result in praise, glory and honor when Jesus Christ is revealed. (NIV)*

Being sold out to Jesus says your life is no longer consumed by the things of this world but by your relationship and devotion to Him. You have come to know and believe that you will experience far greater satisfaction and peace from Jesus than from any loss that could occur in this world. The things of this world no longer bring you the satisfaction they once did. **The only thing that brings satisfaction is an ever-expanding knowledge and experience of who Jesus is.**

POSITIONING LIKE A CHILD

"Get your ducks in a row, and then do it." "Get an education first and then pursue your dream." "You are too old to begin that now, try something that you can do now." "Get your finances in order first." None of these admonishments are wrong, but all can prevent God's work in your life. God often puts us in situations for which we are ill-equipped. Instead of obeying, we begin to filter God's leading through the eyes of the world. Moses famously did this when God called him to lead the Jewish people out of Egypt. As you read Moses' and God's conversations in Exodus 3 and 4, think of a personal situation where you are struggling to step out in faith.

- Exodus 3:11 Moses asked God, *'Who am I, that I should go to Pharaoh and bring the Israelites out of Egypt?'* (NIV) To which God replied in Exodus 3:14, *"This is what you are to say to the Israelites: "I AM has sent me to you."'* (NIV) God might pick you to do something that you consider yourself least likely to do, but *God (I AM WHO I AM)* is the one who will do it.
- Exodus 4:1 The Moses asked, *'What if they do not believe me or listen to me?'* (NIV) To which God replied in Exodus 4:2, *'What is that in your hand?'* (NIV) As God could use an ordinary staff for His work through Moses, so He can use the ordinary in your life to showcase not your hand, but God's hand at work.
- Exodus 4:10 Moses complained, *'O Lord, I have never been eloquent, neither in the past nor since you have spoken to your servant. I am slow of speech and tongue.'* (NIV) To which God replied in Exodus 4:11-12, *'Who gave man his mouth? Who makes him deaf or mute? Who gives him sight or makes him blind? Is it not I, the LORD? Now go;*

I will help you speak and will teach you what to say.' (NIV) God, the Creator, who made the heavens, the universe, the earth and all that is in them is more than able to use the talents with which He has equipped you.

- Exodus 4:13 Moses begged, *'O Lord, please send someone else to do it.'* (NIV) To which God replied in Exodus 4:15, *'I will help both (Moses and Aaron – Moses' brother) of you speak and will teach you what to do.'* (NIV) Moses finally comes to the crux of what he had been struggling with - He preferred not to speak to Pharaoh because of fear. In all this Moses was still not comprehending that it was God who would do it, and not him. **What God desires to do through you is not meant to uplift you, but to uplift the God of gods, the King of kings, the Lord of Lords!**

The Christian life is a faith walk that is dependent on believing and trusting God. Your ability to believe and trust God is often rooted in how you feel about yourself. You know your limitations; you know the areas of your life where Jesus is not Lord; you know the things you value more than anything and anyone else. Your faith problem stems from your unwillingness to respond in obedience to God. Jesus knows your human weaknesses and bluntly said in Luke 18:17 that you would never experience the Christian life unless you were willing to become like a little child, *'I tell you the truth, anyone who will not receive the kingdom of God like a little child will never enter it.'* (NIV) As adults we desire knowledge, understanding, and control to make decisions, while a child acts out of faith and innocence. **Luke 18:17 explains you do not need all the information tied down, but you need only to trust God for the results.** Your problem is not that you can't, but that you are not willing to give up control and trust God.

Your human weaknesses give you the opportunity to trust Christ for what you are going through so that you can see and experience the hand of God at work. When you submit to God in your point of weakness, you are actually strongest, because you have transferred your circumstances to God, the Maker of heaven and earth. How exciting to experience firsthand God's work in your life! 2 Corinthians 12:9-10 conveys how your weakness provides God the opportunity to be God:

> *But He said to me, 'My grace is sufficient for you, for My power is made perfect in weakness.' Therefore I will boast all the more gladly about my weaknesses, so that Christ's power may rest on me. That is why, for Christ's sake, I delight in weaknesses, in insults, in hardships, in persecutions, in difficulties. For when I am weak, then I am strong. (NIV)*

A child has no pretensions of his weaknesses and strengths, but only the desire and faith to act. **If you want to experience God; if you want God to work through your life; if you want God to be the sustenance of your life, you must live your life with the faith of a child.** Believe He is God and trust Him. Do not consider the world's evaluation of the situation. Let God be God and you be His child. **Take the position of a child and God will take the position of your heavenly Father who knows what is best for you.** God will work His chosen purpose through you. Romans 8:28 gives you the assurance that God works for your good: *And we know that in all things God works for the good of those who love Him, who have been called according to His purpose. (NIV)*

POSITIONING IN HUMILITY

Jesus picked the analogy of the eye of the needle to amplify that those Christians who position themselves as the least and weakest rather than the most powerful are in the best positions to be used by God. **As pride is the gateway to sin, so humility is the gateway for more of God in your life.** The Jews expectantly waited for a king who would triumphantly redeem the nation of Israel. They did not expect Jesus, a common man, who claimed to be God in human form. One of the most distinguishing character traits of Jesus was humility. Jesus associated with the untouchables, the sinners, the poor, groups He should not have associated with, the diseased, and the despised people of power. Jesus associated with these people not only to proclaim the gospel to all, but also because they were the most receptive. Jesus could have easily aligned Himself with the rich, powerful, important, and influential, but He knew those in need would be more receptive to the gospel than those who saw sufficiency in their abundance, stature, and position.

Isaiah 57:15 shows how God thrives not among the greatest, but the least:

> *For this is what the high and lofty One says — He who lives forever, whose name is holy: 'I live in a high and holy place, but also with him who is contrite and lowly in spirit, to revive the spirit of the lowly and to revive the heart of the contrite.'* (NIV)

When you walk in humility, you begin to dwell in the Holy Place of God. Humility makes you available to God not only for the crafting of Godly character and greater spiritual purpose, but also for His greatest work. **Pride pushes God away while humility creates a vacuum that takes you into the deepest places of the kingdom**

of God. This is why Isaiah 66:2 proclaims: *This is the one I esteem: he who is humble and contrite in spirit, and trembles at My word.* (NIV) This is contrary to the way of the world. The world esteems greatness, but God esteems the humble. God's best work is manifested in the humble, not the brightest, strongest, and most powerful. God's power is displayed best out of one's weakness and humility. **Humility is an incredible position because it places you at the pinnacle of God's handiwork.** What an unbelievable position humility is, knowing that it is synonymous with God's esteem for you! Psalm 118:8-9 describes the position of the humble who trust more in God than man: *It is better to take refuge in the LORD than to trust in man. It is better to take refuge in the LORD than to trust in princes.* (NIV)

POSITIONING BY BEING LAST

Humility has a major drawback - it takes you out of the race for first. Or does it? Jesus reordered our world when He taught in Matthew 20:16, *'So the last will be first, and the first will be last.'* (NIV) I love playing with my grandson. We make everything a race: going to the car, swimming, racquetball, dressing, and eating. Upon finishing each competition, we each exclaim "I won! I am the champion." This always ends up with both laughing and trying to talk ourselves into being first. A few weeks ago he said, "Poppy, we can both be champions and winners." In retrospect, I wish I had said it first, but I was too busy trying to be first! Sometimes it takes a child to teach us. Winning is engrained in every aspect of life. We are driven to win at sports, perform at work in order to get the promotion, and to always be first. God's way is quite different. In God's eyes, each individual has incalculable importance — we are all champions, no matter the differences, abilities, or positions in life. **In God's economy, it is not what you do as much as what**

God does in you. How many opportunities do you miss by being first? Being at the head of the line causes you to miss all the needs of people behind you. From the front you cannot see those who are hurting, those who need help, and those who need encouragement, but only the view of yourself. Our desire for being first often leaves God totally out. Instead of walking through life with God, we are busy squashing others to get to the front. Instead of being used by God, we are oblivious to the needs of those around us. Being first takes you out of the important position of being available to be used by God in the lives of those behind you. As God becomes first and others become second, you will begin to enjoy the wonderful vantage point of not only seeing all that is happening around you, but also experiencing a greater work of God. **You may be last in the eyes of the world, but you will be first in the eyes of God.**

POSITIONING BY SERVING

The final position for the eye of the needle is serving. As Jesus prepared for the end of His life, He did not focus on succession planning, correct doctrine, or a strategic plan; His focus was serving. At the Last Supper, Jesus got in front of His disciples to give His last major address, not with great oratory, but by example. One by one, Jesus removed the sandals of each of His disciples and began washing their feet. Jesus explained His actions in John 13:14-15,

> *'Now that I, your Lord and Teacher, have washed your feet, you also should wash one another's feet. I have set you an example that you should do as I have done for you.' (NIV)*

Action supersedes words. You can preach to people all day long, but actions have far greater impact. Your words can reflect your heart, but your mind, emotions, and flesh can easily pollute the message. God can amplify His and your heart far more effectively in service to others. Jesus wanted to vividly convey the importance of serving, because He knew it was a foundational building block for the disciples carrying forth His life and message. **If you want to be an effective follower of Christ, serve!**

In John 12:26 Jesus tells how you can serve Him, *'Whoever serves Me must follow Me; and where I am, My servant also will be. My Father will honor the one who serves Me.'* (NIV) This verse reveals three important steps to empowering yourself to serve. First is to dwell intimately in Jesus' presence. Second is to learn how to serve by following Jesus' example. Third is to obey the commands of Jesus.

Serve others if you truly want to serve Jesus. Serving is the emptying of self for the benefit of others. Serving not only embodies most of the positions we have already talked about, but also the full character and love of Christ. The most beautiful description of a servant was of Jesus in Philippians 2:6-8:

> *Who being in very nature God, did not consider equality with God something to be grasped, but made Himself nothing, taking the very nature of a servant, being made in human likeness. And being found in appearance as a man, He humbled Himself and became obedient to death — even death on a cross! (NIV)*

If you want more of Jesus, empty yourself for the service of others. Life is not about you, but about Jesus. 1 Corinthians 8:1b tells how words without action can have the opposite effect: *Knowledge puffs up, but love builds up.* (NIV) What greater way of building up another than by serving them?

Early on in Jesus' ministry, the disciples of John the Baptist were concerned about Jesus' ministry encroaching on theirs. John the

Baptist was faced with the decision to continue leading his ministry or to serve Jesus. John replied to his disciples in John 3:30, '*He (Jesus) must become greater; I must become less.*' (NIV) John's ministry was never about serving himself, but serving God. John knew Scripture and prophecy and understood that his role was to serve Jesus, not compete with Him. How easy it is to be serving Jesus while slowly moving towards a ministry serving yourself. **A follower of Christ represents God above self. A servant puts others as well as everything in his life ahead of himself for the benefit of others.** This description of serving vividly portrays the best of the positions we have studied, because it replicates what God did for us in Jesus, who *made Himself nothing, taking the very nature of a servant.*

How are you positioned to serve God in these nine areas? Your words may echo commitment, your heart may pound for Jesus, but **have you positioned your life beyond God's reach**? Put off the old self where your position opposes God's desires for you. Positioning is critical for going through the eye of the needle. You may be positioned poorly in one or many of these areas, but each must be consecrated to God. **Every area of your life is meant to be surrendered into God's hands. A willing heart that is imprisoned in the self-absorbed positions of one's life is of little use to God. This is like fruit that is rotting on the vine. It is not enough to want God's best, but you must position yourself for God's best.**

FIVE

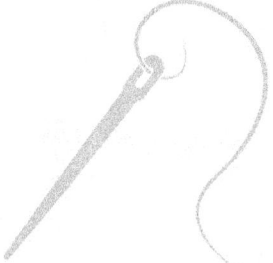

What is Blocking Me?

NOW THAT YOU ARE POSITIONED for going through the eye of the needle, what is stopping you? Or, should I say, what is blocking you? Your life in Jesus is not a smorgasbord of taking what you like and ignoring what you do not like. God wants to envelop your life into His so that you can experience all He has for you. Chapter 2, "Where Am I?", helped you understand who God is in your life and the corrupted beliefs that might be thwarting God's work. This chapter will help you identify specific areas of your life where you have chosen unrighteousness instead of righteousness, the world before Jesus, your desires instead of God's desires, your friends over Jesus, your possessions over the most valuable possession you can have, a relationship with Jesus. You cannot go through the eye of the needle when your life is consumed with things that come before Jesus.

Being a Christian sounds great until God starts getting in your way. You have heard many of God's promises and desire to see them actualized in you. Unfortunately, God's work to bring those promises into reality will begin to conflict with the life you live. You will have to confront the obstacles that are blocking God if you are to experience all that He has for you. This collision of your life with God's desires is not bad, but it needs to be worked through to prevent your ways from blocking God's way. You block God's ways by allowing sin to rule your life. The problem with this is that you are not just blocking God's design for you and what God wants for you; you are also blocking God Himself. God chooses to work through a willing and available life, but God always has the power to override man's choices. God's will is broader than your desires. God's will includes His purposes for you, around you, and in the broader world itself.

Here are two stories of people blocking God as they contemplate sin over God:

- A Christian who had been married for fifteen years began experiencing marital problems that were a repeat of problems he worked through in the past. The exasperation of having to deal with the same problems while ignoring the agreed-upon remedies pushed him to start justifying divorcing his wife. As I talked with him, I began to sense that the purpose of the conversation was not to find solutions to his marital problems, but to get support for leaving his wife. I said, "John (fictional name), do not even go there. It is far easier to work through these issues than to remain single for the rest of your life." I could see the shock on his face upon hearing this. I explained there is no remarriage in divorce except for adultery. He needed to quit focusing on sin (considering divorce) and focus on how to resolve the issues in his marriage. This story ended well. The next time we met, his relationship had substantially improved. Instead of focusing on divorce, which the world considers the remedy for difficult marriage problems, he recommitted to his covenant of marriage, trusted God, and began resolving the issues in his marriage.

- A 38-year-old man had struggled for 25 years with addiction. Part of his addicted lifestyle included promiscuity. The man had been a Christian from early childhood yet had struggled with an addicted lifestyle most of his life. As we talked about his recovery, he shared with me what God was doing and how God had rescued him from his drug addiction. He was on track for a remarkable spiritual transformation until he began a new relationship that had progressed too quickly. Fortunately, he had already recognized that he had yielded to sin and needed to slow down. He then explained that as long as he strived for purity, there was forgiveness in failure, which was true. Unfortunately, he had begun premeditating his sexual sins knowing that God would forgive him. Our relationship with God is not like a game of chess. God is God, sin is sin, and sin has consequences. Sin starts in the heart. This young man was trying to manage sin in the flesh while preparing for failure. His focus should have been the heart, protecting self, and focusing on God's redemptive power to protect, rescue, and satisfy. Instead he contemplated, and then chose, to become vulnerable to sin instead of going deeper into the heart of God. Does God continue to prosper a person with this mindset? How does his sin affect other areas of his life? How is his fellowship with God affected by his sin? His choices may very well begin to block God's great work in his life.

I could give many more examples of how Christians choose to block God through their actions, beliefs, and contortions of the truth. These blockers are not so much individual sins, but sin patterns that produce or lead to sin. Anytime your lifestyle begins to block God you are robbing yourself of the opportunity to experience what God has for you. As you read this chapter, be aggressive in challenging yourself about anything that may be blocking God's work in you. When you identify a blocker in your life, immediately record it, pray about it, ask God how you are to deal with it, and then take action. Do not be a James 1:23-24 Christian:

Anyone who listens to the word but does not do what it says is like a man who looks at his face in a mirror and, after looking at himself, goes away and immediately forgets what he looks like.

Rather, be a James 1:25 Christian:

But the man who looks intently into the perfect law that gives freedom, and continues to do this, not forgetting what he has heard, but doing it — he will be blessed in what he does. (NIV)

You will begin to change the attitude of your mind as you identify and change blockers in your life. Ephesians 4:23 tells you: *to be made new in the attitude of your minds. (NIV)*

IS JESUS MY LORD?

Making Jesus Lord of your life is one of the foundational requirements for coming to salvation in Christ. Making Jesus Lord is easier professed at salvation than lived out in your daily life. Making Jesus Lord is like breathing. Every activity, thought, and goal is like taking in a breath. The question is what will you breathe out? Will you exhale what you want or what Jesus wants? Will you exhale what feels good or trust Jesus for your circumstances? Will you exhale what produces the least pain and discomfort or let God take you where He wants? Will you choose what makes the most money or what produces the greatest results in the kingdom of God? Will you choose the things of this world that produce temporal happiness or the joy that Jesus gives you? **Your life as a Christian is like learning how to breathe. Each breath you take in gives you another opportunity to hear God, to experience Him as God, to learn patience, and to learn more of His way and truth. You breathe out by obediently following God.**

In Job 11:13-17 Jophar explains how to seek and obey God as the Lord of your life,

'Yet if you devote your heart to Him and stretch out your hands to Him, if you put away the sin that is in your hand and allow no evil to dwell in your tent, then you will lift up your face without shame; you will stand firm and without fear. You will surely forget your trouble, recalling it only as waters gone by. Life will be brighter than noonday, and darkness will become like morning.' (NIV)

Let's break down this passage of Scripture:

This Scripture begins with Lordship, *"Devote your heart to Him."* Who or what your heart is devoted to is the Lord of your life. Filtering everything through your Lordship to God puts His fingerprints on your life. That from which you exclude God does not have His fingerprints, and it also lacks God's fulfilling purpose. Pray continually for any area where you are in control and not God, so that you can obediently be pruning your life.

'Stretch out your hands to Him' speaks to your desire and efforts. Seldom does anything come in life without desire or effort. Do you desire God's hand in your life in the same way you desire the things of this world?

Let me give two examples:

1. Would you be willing to pursue God with the same diligence that you pursue an education? A college education normally includes thirteen years for your high school diploma and four for your college degree. Would it be unrealistic to give that much time to God? This would be a huge commitment, but who is Lord of your life?

2. Now an example with lesser commitment. In discipling others, I encourage Scripture memory of the key verses that God puts in a person's life for repentance, transformation, meditation, and training. Memorize those verses that God is pressing into your heart. I show people that Scripture memory takes little time when done during times of waiting. Are you willing to give God a little more of your time, effort, and heart to experience more of Him? The other day I met for lunch with one of the men I disciple. Part of our discipling time is to recite any new Scriptures memorized along with what God was impressing on his heart. He said he had not memorized anything new, because life was so busy. During our meeting I left the table for five minutes. When I returned, he was playing a game on his phone. He had made a conscious decision to devote five minutes of free time to playing a phone game. With a changed priority and desire, he could have used this five minutes to fulfill his commitment to memorize Scripture. Are you willing to make Jesus the Lord

of your life enough to 'stretch out your hands to Him,' so that you can receive all that He has for you?

'Put away the sin that is in your hand' speaks to known sin in your life. We all have sin in our lives. A life that is unaware of sin is a life that is not dwelling in the Lord in a consistent, deep way. The deeper you go into cultivating a relationship with God, the more His holiness will illuminate sin in your life. Once sin is revealed, you have a decision to continue in sin or to get rid of it. Do you love God enough to make Him Lord by being willing to ask Him to help you put away any sin in your life? God is willing and able to walk with you in gaining victory over sin.

'Allow no evil to dwell in your tent' speaks to your environment. You will experience more of God if you make the life you live fertile for God. On the other hand, you will be pulled down, compromised, or made ineffective if you allow sin and temptation to constantly inhabit your environment. Making Jesus Lord releases the Holy Spirit to show you the areas of life that can pull you down rather than build you up in Christ. Allowing your environment to be fertile ground for Christ provides rich soil for allowing a victorious life in Christ. Allow the tent of your life to draw you into Lordship, not away from it.

'You will lift up your face without shame.' Making Jesus Lord allows Him to remove the junk in your life that is blocking God. This allows you to have increasingly unfettered fellowship and communication with God. Your heart, mind, and conscience will be better aligned to experience God in all His glory, might, and love. Instead of experiencing the failure and shame of sin, you now live a life that reflects and experiences more of Christ while pointing others to Him.

'You will stand firm and without fear.' As you trust God, you will

experience more of Him. Your growing relationship and experience with God will help you know Him better as well as give you an increasing fortitude that helps you stand firm without fear.

'You will surely forget your trouble, recalling it only as waters gone by.' This points to a life lived under the Lordship of Christ. Putting Jesus first in your life and growing in your faith all point to a life that has made Jesus Lord. Making Jesus Lord allows you to place your troubles in God's hands. **Lordship is letting God be in control so that you can see the hand of God at work.**

'Life will be brighter than noonday, and darkness will become like morning.' This describes the fruit of Lordship. Whether things are good, average, or bad, your life will be great in the hands of God. Romans 8:28 gives you the hope and confidence of living life by trusting God: *We know that God causes all things to work together for good to those who love God, to those who are called according to His purpose.* (NASB)

Making Jesus Lord gives God greater access to your life. Allowing God to more freely work in you lets your relationship with God flourish. **Lordship frees the Spirit to operate with power and direction.** Lordship moves you toward the loving relationship God desires with you. Begin each day by proclaiming Him Lord of your life. Ask Jesus to fill you with His Spirit and to guide you through your day.

DO I LOVE RIGHTEOUSNESS?

God loves righteousness, obedience, and Godly living. Christians are reminded by Jesus in Luke 10:27 to, *'Love the Lord your God with all your heart and with all your soul and with all your strength and with all your mind. . .'* (NIV) Jesus teaches in John 14:21 that you show your love for God by obedience, *'Whoever has My commands and obeys them, he is the one who loves Me.'* (NIV) This does not mean God does not love the disobedient, but just as a parent has special affection for their children when they obey, so your heavenly Father has special affection for His children when they are obedient. This special affection is not only for being obedient, but also knowing their life will be better. Your heavenly Father always has your best interests at heart in both good and bad circumstances. Obedience leads to righteousness and God loves righteousness.

In John 14:23 Jesus explains how obedience leads you into God's heart, resulting in righteousness, *'If anyone loves Me, he will obey My teaching. My Father will love him, and We will come to him and make our home with him.'* (NIV) Knowing you can come more into God's joy should provide a strong desire for obedience. The problem with obedience is that you live in a sinful body and environment that constantly pulls you toward sin. Trying to overcome the temptations that thwart obedience can subtly lead you to working for obedience in the flesh rather than in God's power. Obedience in the flesh will not only be filled with inconsistencies and contradictions to righteousness, but it will also be counter-productive to loving God. Learning to love God will come more naturally as you learn to love righteousness.

Obedience flows naturally when you love righteousness. Your love for righteousness will grow in direct proportion to the depth of your relationship with Christ. This has been stated in multiple ways throughout this book. At this point, you may say that all the things desired in your Christian life will flow out of your relationship with Christ. Yes! Romans 8:28 shows what happens to those who love God: *And we know that in all things God works for the good of those who love Him, who have been called according to His purpose.* (NIV) My point is that if you want to love righteousness, you must love God. God is righteousness. You cannot separate the two, nor can you make a formula for living by focusing only on righteousness. Our focus must always be on loving God. Your love for God will grow in proportion to your investment in God. Is this not true in all of life? What you value and receive depends on what you invest. All too often we invest far more in the things of this world than we do in God. This is why it is said that **your love for righteousness reveals your heart.**

As your love for righteousness grows, you begin, as explained in Hebrews 5:12-14, to move from living your Christian life on milk to living it on solid food:

> . . .*You need milk, not solid food! Anyone who lives on milk, being still an infant, is not acquainted with the teaching about righteousness. But solid food is for the mature, who by constant use have trained themselves to distinguish good from evil. (NIV)*

This shift from milk to solid food, and the growth that accompanies it, feeds your love for righteousness. Instead of a shallow faith, your faith deepens as you apply God's truths. Instead of allowing sin to continue blocking the transformation of your mind, heart, and soul, you become more captivated by the wonder and experience of God's righteousness. Your growing love for righteousness will free the Holy Spirit to increase your discernment while sharpening your senses to fight and perceive evil. 2 Peter 1:5-9 illustrates the transition that occurs from a life entrapped by the world to an ever-increasing love for righteousness:

> *For this very reason, make every effort to add to your faith goodness; and to goodness, knowledge; and to knowledge,*

> *self-control; and to self-control, perseverance; and to perseverance, godliness; and to godliness, brotherly kindness; and to brotherly kindness, love. For if you possess these qualities in increasing measure, they will keep you from being ineffective and unproductive in your knowledge of our Lord Jesus Christ. But if anyone does not have them, he is nearsighted and blind, and has forgotten that he has been cleansed from his past sins. (NIV)*

This passage speaks beautifully to transformation because it shows how each step into righteousness leads to a greater step into transformation. Conversely, this is also the way sin works. In Luke 16:10 Jesus describes sin precipitating more sin:

> *'Whoever can be trusted with very little can also be trusted with much, and whoever is dishonest with very little will also be dishonest with much.' (NIV)*

Sin leads to greater sin, while each step of righteousness leads not only to greater righteousness, but also to a greater work of God. How much more fun it is to be caught in a spiral up to righteousness instead of a spiral deeper into sin. Increased sin only multiplies into more sin, while increasing righteousness flourishes from a greater work of God in your life. Spiraling up into righteousness creates hunger and desire for more of God, while sin only brings death to your life. Sin brings death, while righteousness brings life. **The very nature of living in Christ is growth, while sin diminishes you to the point of death.**

Every situation in life at its core is a confrontation with truth. Are you going to choose God's way or the world's way? God's way always chooses righteousness, while the world's ways choose sin.

Allowing God to consume your life in His righteousness brings the great benefit of not only releasing the active work of His life in you, but you also being infused with all the life-giving characteristics of the fruit of the Spirit. Galatians 5:22-23 teaches: *But the fruit of the Spirit is love, joy, peace, patience, kindness, goodness, faithfulness, gentleness and self-control.* (NIV) Continue to pursue God with all your heart, so that as you go deeper into Him, your love for righteousness will grow. Allow your expanding love for righteousness to consume increasing measures of your flesh, the world, and satan's attacks. Enjoy your increasing pleasure in God as described in 1 John 2:5: *But if anyone obeys His word, God's love is truly made complete in Him.* (NIV)

CAPTURING THE FUTURE

A Christian can block Christ in his life by continuing to live in the past. Almost everyone has had agony, hardship, bitterness, unforgiveness, or tragedy at some time in their past. Instead of moving on, people tend to cling to their past. They keep reliving the incident, experiencing the hurt, and obsessing about it. One gentleman I discipled carried deep scars from sexual abuse in the past. He shared these tragic events early on in our discipling relationship. They had been dealt with and forgiveness had been extended and accepted from the offender. A few weeks later during a discipling session, he emotionally and loudly commented on an abuse that occurred early in life. I asked him why he was bringing it up? He replied, "What you said was a trigger." I explained to him that he had dealt with the issue and forgiven the offender, so it was behind him. He agreed, but said he just had to respond to the trigger. This is so common in people who are hurting. **They refuse to let go of the past because it is almost like a pacifier, keeping them from**

living for today. The Lord speaks in Isaiah 43:18-19 how clinging to the past can block God's work in the present,

> *'Forget the former things; do not dwell on the past. See, I am doing a new thing! Now it springs up; do you not perceive it? I am making a way in the desert and streams in the wasteland.' (NIV)*

Either you believe God's promises, ignore them, or you deny them. Believing and stepping into God's promises opens your life to God doing a new thing. Continuing to regress into the past takes you back to the desert and wasteland that originally hurt you. There is no life in the desert and wasteland. Your choice is to live in the past or embrace God in the present. Your choice is highly influenced by the depth of your relationship with Jesus. Continually regressing into the past is indicative of a shallow relationship with Christ. A deeper walk with Christ takes you deeper into the heart of God, allowing healing and reconciliation to take place. It is important not to stop there; allow healing and reconciliation to let you see God's work through your past experiences, while forgiving and, at times, having compassion for the offender. Many times, offenders in your life are only acting out of the offenses that have been perpetuated on them in the past. Allow God to use you in their lives to break them free of their bondages.

Allow God to use your past experiences to mature and grow you so that you can be a light to God's redemptive power in you and others. Continuing to live your life in the past will have a neutralizing effect on your life in Christ. It is difficult for God to work in your life while you are clinging to past hurts. Do not allow your past hurts to block God's work in the present and paralyze your future.

2 Corinthians 5:17 affirms you: *Therefore, if anyone is in Christ,*

he is a new creation; the old has gone, the new has come! (NIV) Embrace your new life - quit clinging to the past. Living in the past gives satan free rein to torment you. Satan will challenge your salvation, your worth, and your position in Christ. A life that constantly lives in the past is a life that is walking in quicksand. You will be constantly sucked into mires that will destroy the fruit God desires in your life. The longer you stay in the quicksand of your past, the further more you will be pulled into your old life. Psalm 40:2-3, 4 describes the transformation that occurs by making God your trust:

> *He lifted me out of the slimy pit, out of the mud and mire; He set my feet on a rock and gave me a firm place to stand. He put a new song in my mouth, a hymn of praise to our God. . . Blessed is the man who makes the LORD his trust, who does not look to the proud, to those who turn aside to false gods. (NIV)*

Affirm Christ, His work, and His power to not only save, but also to forgive you, redeem your past, and transform you. **Forget the past, get out of the mud pits of life, and fully stand on the solid rock of Christ.**

BIG, BAD SELF

In Matthew 6:24, Jesus lays out an imperative,

> *'No one can serve two masters; for either he will hate the one and love the other, or he will hold to one and despise the other. You cannot serve God and mammon.' (NASB)*

Whom you serve will determine the priorities of your life. Serving

God will cause your priorities to change as well as what each priority will look like. You block God's work in every area where you serve self. Self is like a cancer. Allowing self to gain a foothold in an area of life will weaken and tempt the areas around it.

I knew a Christian man who fell in love with a non-Christian woman. He knew the fact she was not a Christian was a problem, but he let his emotions lead. Notice the devolution of this Christian's life as he continued in the relationship:

- He held the belief that as they grew in relationship she would become a Christian and would grow into similar spiritual beliefs. This was the first corrupted belief: It is okay to be unequally yoked.
- She was a lot of fun and loved to party. They began to party constantly. Partying consisted of excessive drinking, occasional drugs, and frequenting venues that only reinforced this type of lifestyle. The second corrupted belief: participating in small sins and compromises will help build a stronger relationship that will make it easier to engage her spiritually with the Gospel message of salvation.
- Since they had nothing in common in terms of faith, he minimized the spiritual involvement in their relationship so as not to alienate her. The third corrupted belief: she will be more drawn to Christ by never mentioning Him or sharing truths that should have guided their relationship. He did not want to pressure her, but thought she could be won over through their relationship and his example.
- They got engaged and marriage preparations were taking increasing amounts of time, making it difficult for him to dedicate any time to spiritual stimulation, Christian fellowship, and spiritual growth. The fourth corrupted belief: in the future there will be more time to give to God.

- The intimacy of their relationship led to sexual involvement. The fifth corrupted belief: they were getting married anyway, so what is wrong with premarital sex? Sin begets sin.

Each of these corrupted beliefs would have been stopped up front if only the man served God first instead of himself. Putting self before God almost always leads to a slippery slope of increasing sin. **As you put self before God, you are asking God to stand down as you take over the reins of your life.** As you make yourself Lord of your life, you increasingly block God, which naturally attracts more compromise and sin.

Serving self is often guided by pride. Prideful self says: "I know better than God. I can violate God's truths and principles because I can control the outcomes. I am strong enough to not fall into temptation and sin." James 4:6 describes this as a dangerous place: *'God opposes the proud but gives grace to the humble.'* (NIV) The prideful are more than disobeying and blocking God; they are actually going to war with God. God does not just relent to the proud but opposes them. While God is pressing correction into your life, you are blocking Him and the righteousness He desires for you. Prideful self is metaphorically lifting a shield that is blocking God's work, input, and desires for you. You may continue to desire God and His life, but you are simultaneously telling God to stay away because you think you know what is best for you and have no need for Him. The things of God that you agree with you accept, but the things of God that run contrary to self - you reject.

The other problem with pride is that you begin living life in the sufficiency of self. You are not only telling God you are okay in handling your life, but that you are quite capable of doing it. **Sufficiency in self is the way of the world, while God's way is realizing your deficiency without Him. Sufficiency sidelines God,**

while deficiency allows God to step in and thrive. 2 Corinthians 12:10 says your best comes out of your weakness because God's power is made perfect in weakness: *That is why, for Christ's sake, I delight in weakness, in insults, in hardships, in persecutions, in difficulties. For when I am weak, then I am strong.* (NIV) **If you want the active work of God, you must stand down so that He can stand up in your life.**

You are a new creation in Christ, but you still live in a body that has many sin habits that have been cultivated over the years. The propensity of your old self is still to sin which continues to block God. Jeremiah 17:9 should kill any thought that self can bring fruit in the kingdom of God: *The heart is deceitful above all things and beyond cure.* (NIV) If you want more of God turn away from self. Ask God's help in the areas of life where you have replaced Him. Unleash the powerful work of the Holy Spirit by humbling yourself before God; in this way He can extend more grace. Remove the barriers you have placed between God and you as James 4:10 instructs: *Humble yourselves before the Lord, and He will lift you up.* (NIV)

GOD'S GOLD

Gold immediately draws your thoughts to money and wealth. Money is a part of God's gold, but His gold is any treasure in your life. **God wants to possess your heart so that it beats to His heart.** Jesus teaches in Matthew 6:19-21 that anything that captures your heart is the treasure of your life. Any treasure apart from God's treasure will pull your heart from God:

'Do not lay up for yourselves treasures upon earth, where moth and rust destroy, and where thieves break in and steal. But lay up for yourselves treasures in heaven, where neither

moth nor rust destroys, and where thieves do not break in or steal; for where your treasure is, there will your heart be also.' (NASB)

God wants to be the treasure of your life. As your life is consumed into God's, His life will be released to you in greater portions. Any area of life that you have made your earthly treasure blocks God and ultimately thwarts His work in that area. Here are some of the treasures in your life that might be blocking God: Money, relationships, sports, smart phones, television, games, activities, hobbies, work, music, kid's activities, and anything else that is happening apart from God.

For the most part, none of your treasures, practiced in moderation and prudence, are bad in themselves. They only become bad when you elevate them above God which blocks Him and thwarts His work in those areas. God wants to come first. He wants to be your treasure in every area of your life.

Some treasures are subtler in their nature. Movies and television are not bad in themselves or when watched in moderation and in balance with your life's callings. They became your treasure when their excess relegates God's relationship and work to the back of the line. These can also become your treasures when their content takes precedence over God's righteousness. Lowering your standards to be comfortable with sin says entertainment and pleasure is more important than God, His ways, and His desires for you. Pornography, soft porn, active promotion of non-Biblical lifestyles, and language all fall into this category. Jesus explains Matthew 6:22-23 how your life can be degraded by what you take in,

'The lamp of the body is the eye; if therefore your eye is clear, your whole body will be full of light. But if your eye is

bad, your whole body will be full of darkness. If therefore the light that is in you is darkness, how great is the darkness!' (NASB)

Another subtle area that can draw you away from God might be the technology of smartphones. These wonderful devices can quickly replace God, relationships, priorities, spiritual growth, and family. What is the ratio of time spent on your smartphone compared to time spent with God, your family, or priorities?

Smartphones have become a parade of interruptions and time consumption that sap your life away. Would you allow your life to be arbitrarily consumed each day by a parade of people performing different acts to catch your attention? Imagine an array of uninvited entertainers showing up at your home throughout the day to play with your kids. How productive would you be if people kept showing up to play games that you enjoy? What would the quality of your work be if newsmen, market analysts, and weathermen kept breaking in with their latest updates? Could you ever get a focus on life if you were constantly being interrupted by people telling you trivial, entertaining, humorous stories? Can you even begin to imagine 100 people showing up every day in an uncontrolled way to rob your life of time, emotion, concentration, and direction outside of God's will and purpose?

Look around and see how people are glued to their phones or other electronic devices. Watch how many people are playing with their phones during church, or how many tables of people in restaurants are on their devices while ignoring spouses, friends, and kids. Observe how family members are on electronic devices instead of interacting, raising children, and pursuing meaningful life. The balance between technology and living a life purposefully for God is delicate, but one that needs to be maintained. Answering the question of whether God or the smartphone controls your life will help you better align your life with God. Allowing the smartphone to be Lord of your life leaves little time for your spouse, children, duties in life, work, gratifying events to attend, creative learning and entertainment with those you love. The smartphone can replace your quiet time with God, time for going deeper with God, and time for ministry.

In Luke 12:20-21, Jesus shows the futility and emptiness of making other things your treasures in this parable,

"But God said to him, "You fool! This very night your life will be demanded from you. Then who will get what you have prepared for yourself?" This is how it will be with anyone who stores up things for himself but is not rich toward God.' (NIV)

What are the treasures in your life? Look at your activities, how you spend your money, where you give your money, and how you spend your time. Some are required for living, but many desires represent what you want rather than what God wants. Prayerfully analyzing these areas will reveal where God has been replaced by your treasures. If God holds a high place of importance, adequate time will be devoted to Him. Examining your life will also help expose areas of sin that you treasure. It will be difficult for God to flourish in any area where sin is your treasure. Confront sin head on through confession and restoration. Allow God to replace or take hold of any area where you have pushed Him aside. Embrace God as your gold…your very great reward. Allow everything to flow out of your relationship with Jesus.

TRUST BUSTERS

Matthew 6:25-32: 'For this reason I say to you, do not be anxious for your life, as to what you shall eat, or what you shall drink; nor for your body, as to what you shall put on. Is not life more than food, and the body more than clothing? Look at the birds of the air, that they do not sow, neither do they reap, nor gather into barns, and yet your heavenly Father feeds them. Are you not worth much more than they? And which of you being anxious can add a single cubit to his life's span? And why are you anxious about clothing?
Observe how the lilies of the field grow; they do not toil nor do they spin, yet I say to you that even Solomon in all his glory did not clothe himself like one of these. But if God so arrays the grass of the field, which is alive today and tomorrow is thrown into the furnace, will He not much more do so for you, O men of little faith? Do not be anxious then, saying, "What shall we eat?" or "What shall we drink?" Or "With what shall we clothe ourselves?" For all these things the Gentiles eagerly seek; for your heavenly Father knows that you need all these things.' (NASB)

Life can swiftly be reduced to a kettle of anxiety. There is very little you cannot take to a point of anxiety. Every anomaly that happens around your house or in your car can create fear of something possibly going wrong. Every person you interact with has an opinion of you; "Yikes, surely they cannot think that!" "What if the government does this?" "What will happen if that person is elected?" "Money is tight." "Is my job secure?" "What if the economy goes south? I will be financially destitute if this happens." But remember what Jesus said in Mathew 6:26, '*Look at the birds of the air, that they do not sow, neither do they reap, nor gather into barns, and yet your heavenly Father feeds them.'* (NASB) Any of these situations can unsettle your life if you process them outside of the kingdom of God.

In Matthew 6:33 Jesus directs you in dealing with life's challenges, *'But seek first His kingdom and His righteousness, and all these things will be given to you as well.'* (NIV) Your focus in life changes from provisions, relationships, and the things of this world to trusting God with your well-being. It might look bleak, but the same God who cares for the sparrows and clothes the lilies of the field will also provide for you. **God's provision may look different from the provision you desire, but trusting Him moves you from being consumed by the circumstance to trusting Him for the result.**

Failing to trust God blocks or hinders His work in you. Anxiety, worry, and fretfulness are a byproduct of not trusting God. As your life in Christ grows, so will your ability to trust Him. **Each time you trust God, your faith will grow, which prepares you for greater steps of faith.** Conversely, your faith will dwindle if you continually fail to trust God. Instead of trusting God and stepping out in His power and glory, you play by the world's rules resulting in the emptiness of the world. 2 Samuel 22:37 speaks of the benefits of trusting God: *You gave a wide place for my steps under me, and my feet did not slip.* (ESV) Each step of faith allows God to enlarge your faith, giving you firmer footing for your life in this world. **Your faith does not remove difficulties but equips you to navigate them.**

These six blockers can easily stand between you and God. Hopefully the blockers that have been exposed are already starting to dwindle. Do not stop there, spend time asking God to unravel any other blockers in your life.

Ask these six questions:
- Have I made Jesus Lord of every area of my life? Where am I Lord instead of Jesus?
- Do I love righteousness? Does my heart well up in excitement for righteousness? Where is righteousness a downer in my life?
- Are there any areas in the past that are pulling me down?
- Where is self in control? Where has pride pushed God aside?
- What other treasures besides God do I have in my life?
- In what areas of my life do I lack the faith to trust God?

Allow God to expose these blockers in order that you can entrust Him to eradicate them, so that God's life will radiate in and through you. Prayerfully uplift these blockers to God; He can reveal your heart. These blockers begin in the heart. Thus, it is fitting that we will now strengthen the heart with God's truths in the next chapter.

SIX

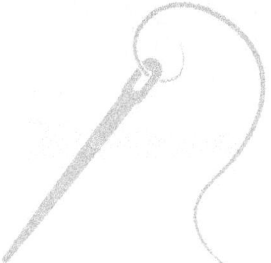

Going Through the Eye of the Needle with Heart

THERE WAS A TIME IN my career when I had the opportunity to start a new business. The opportunity was there, the money needed was available, and people were there to be a part of it. Our culture would say all the stars were aligned for doing it. The only thing missing was heart. I did not have the heart for it. The thrill of a new business was alluring and to be leading and not following was exciting. The possible economic benefits were attractive, but I did not have the heart. Being positioned for something and having the heart to do it are two different things. My heart desired a change from what I had done traditionally to a place that allowed more freedom for Christ in my life. Taking advantage of this opportunity might have satisfied many things in my life, but God was transitioning me to a life of greater ministry, growth, and opportunity. Stepping back and allowing God to speak to me not only helped clarify my heart, but also gave me the freedom to move forward in a calling where my heart was aligned with God.

The same is true in your walk with Christ. Your outward appearance can say you are sold out to Jesus, while your heart says you are not. Hosea 6:6 gives you God's response to a person who says "I love God" but does not have the heart for loving God, *'For I desire mercy, not sacrifice, and acknowledgment of God rather than burnt offerings.'* (NIV) God is saying that all your activities are meaningless without a heart for Him. In the same way it was not enough for the rich man about whom this book was written to say, "I have met all the requirements of the law," or a good church attender to say, "I love God and I attend church every Sunday." God wants your heart and spirit to be broken for Him, so that nothing else comes before Him.

This chapter continues to help your mind to be made new by identifying dark spots in your heart. The following eight characteristics reveal a healthy heart for God. Variations of some of these characteristics have been used in other parts of this book. Do not allow this to distract you from what is being said. This is like a diamond, where each facet can have a different characteristic. As you work through this chapter, ask God to reveal your heart with each characteristic. Allow God to give you a better understanding of what your heart should look like. Let God use each characteristic to till your heart for impurities and opportunities so that your heart might love God more dearly. Remember that as your heart for God grows, you continue to grow smaller. This process allows you to go through the eye of the needle!

UPGRADE FOR FREE

Many convenience stores and restaurants now say you can have the largest size drink for the same price as the small. You can upgrade for free! Faith is similar. God can use the smallest element of faith for huge things. The woman at the well is a great example. Jesus plants a seed, and suddenly she is witnessing about Him to everyone in town. Did I miss Jesus sharing the steps to salvation? Not only does she immediately start telling people about Jesus in her hometown, but she does it in a way that causes some to believe while motivating many others to want to hear from Jesus themselves. Did I miss the two-year program to get trained on being an effective disciple? She had no formal training in what to do with the truth Jesus had given her, how to share it, or the theology behind it. It is common in today's Christian culture for new Christians to refrain from talking about their newfound faith until they have training and have been a Christian for some time. By faith, she immediately shares Christ even before she hears a formal presentation of who Christ is, before she is baptized, before she is taught what Christianity is about, before she goes through new member training, before she is established in the faith, before she joins a small group, and before she has become comfortable with this newfound faith. John 4:39-42 tells what God did with her "measly faith":

> Many of the Samaritans from that town believed in Him (Jesus) because of the woman's testimony. . .So when the Samaritans came to Him, they urged Him to stay with them, and He stayed two days. And because of His words many more became believers. They said to the woman, 'We no longer believe just because of what you said; now we have heard for ourselves, and we know that this man really is the Savior of the world.' (NIV)

The natural tendency of new believers is to say, "I do not know enough to share the good news of Jesus Christ with others." Jesus said in Luke 17:6 that it is not how much you know, but how much you trust in Him,

He (Jesus) replied, "If you have faith as small as a mustard seed, you can say to this mulberry tree, "Be uprooted and planted in the sea," and it will obey you.' (NIV)

Faith is like an upgraded drink. People with the smallest to the largest faith should share the good news of Jesus. God's work in you is not dependent on you, but on the Holy Spirit. God only needs a willing vessel that has the heart to believe and step out in faith.

Your faith is not dependent on knowledge, but upon having a heart to obey and pursue Jesus. Gaining a greater heart for Jesus causes you to exercise your faith. As you continually exercise your faith it will continue to grow, just as the smallest mustard seed grows to the size of a large tree. It is not enough to say you have faith, but do you have the heart to step out in faith? Many a person has declared his great faith in God yet has little faith. In Gethsemane Jesus asked three times for John, James, and Peter to pray that they not fall into temptation. Three times they failed. Earlier Peter resolutely said to Jesus, "I will never desert you," yet later he denied Jesus three times. All twelve disciples loved Jesus, but not one stood by Him when He was arrested. Real faith in Jesus will flow from the heart. In Philippians 2:1 you can almost hear Paul pleading with fellow believers to have even the smallest amount of faith:

If you have any encouragement from being united with Christ, if any comfort from His love, if any fellowship with the Spirit, if any tenderness and compassion. (NIV)

Any faith, even if it is as small as a mustard seed, will ignite Christ in you. Do you have the heart to live your life by faith so that God can be all He desires to be in you?

PEACE

Peace is an essential quality for a follower of Christ. A lack of peace allows the world to suck the life out of your heart making it difficult to live the Christian life. It is like a diesel car that is malfunctioning. Black soot is constantly pouring out of the tailpipe. A heart without peace is constantly pouring out conditions that rob your life of peace: I am not worthy; they failed me before; I cannot do it; that person is better; I am inadequate. Proverbs 14:30 shows how envy effects the heart: *A heart at peace gives life to the body, but envy rots the bones.* (NIV) Envy is not often thought of as sin, but envy is a sin with huge ramifications. A heart that is constantly envying things, others, stature, and activities creates a life with no peace. Constantly desiring more puts you in a perpetual state of dissatisfaction and leaves you with a disintegrating heart instead of the peace promised by Jesus in John 14:27,

> *'Peace I leave with you; My peace I give you. I do not give to you as the world gives. Do not let your hearts be troubled and do not be afraid.' (NIV)*

A heart filled with peace is a heart ready to follow Jesus.

The underlying reason for not having peace is a lack of trust in God. Faith and trust are the bedrock of a follower of Christ. Your walk with Christ has no boundaries without trust and faith. I remember the first trip I took without my parents as a teenager. A friend and I left for California, but we had not yet looked at a road map. Continuing our trip without looking at a map would have left our destination and route without boundaries. **Trusting Christ surrounds your life with the boundary of God's promises. Not trusting Christ opens your life to uncontained anxieties that will drain the life of Christ from your heart.**

A lack of peace is like a yellow caution sign directing you to check your heart with God. Your lack of peace could also be pointing to a shallow relationship with God. Instead of continuing down a road that is riddled with potholes from lack of trust in God, you need to exit those lies. . . learn and believe His promises to you in His Word, so that you can deepen your relationship with God. Most people do the opposite. They accelerate down the path of anxiety, causing their lives to continue to be filled with turmoil. Not only do they accelerate their anxiety, but they also decrease their time with God. Instead of allowing God to fill their heart with the peace He promises in Isaiah 26:3: *You will keep in perfect peace him whose mind is steadfast because he trusts in You. (NIV)*, they pull away from Him causing greater anxiety.

A failure to trust God can also be the result of sin patterns in your life. Some of these sin patterns may have developed over years of following the ways of the world rather than God's way. These patterns of sin have led to a compromised heart that has developed a comfort level of living outside of the way of God. This weakened heart struggles, if not crumbles, when times of squeezing occur. This person's foundation is not based on the truths and promises of God because they have instead chosen what is comfortable and easiest. Instead of proceeding on solid ground, they have proceeded in a way that is murky due to a lifestyle of equivocating with God's truths.

A good friend who had a vibrant life in Christ ended his successful career by relenting to deception and deceit. He was recognized for being a great employee as well as a Christian who was faithful in executing his duties in a Godly manner. Unfortunately, his life from early childhood was filled with repeated deceptions to avoid conflict, protect his pride, and promote his image. These deceptions were small and, for the most part, never harmed anyone. Unfortunately, his life of minor deceptions collided with the truth stated by Jesus in Luke 16:10,

> 'Whoever can be trusted with very little can also be trusted with much, and whoever is dishonest with very little will also be dishonest with much.' (NIV)

His dishonesty ended his career. This sin pattern of dishonesty had become a part of his life in multiple areas without consequence. Regrettably, sin is never static; it continues to grow and consume righteousness. This ambassador for Christ with a righteous reputation became known for dishonesty. This dishonesty flowed from a heart that had become numb to the convictions of the Holy Spirit. What resulted was not only a lost job, but a life that had been lived without peace. The execution of each of these small sins took a toll on his peace. His dishonesty resulted in his life being riddled with anxiety, contradictions, and shame, which fed this sin pattern even more. Sin robs your heart of peace. As you go deeper into Christ, allow Him to reveal your compromises to sin. Confess them, study God's Word and His promises, and ask to be filled with God's truth. Allow God to solidify your heart for Him.

A heart of peace is a heart that beats to the solid rock of Christ, where every wave of life does not consume your faith, but your faith entrusts Christ with every turbulence. Christ, alive in your heart, allows you to place your faith in Him rather than the circumstances at hand. The intersection of difficult situations and trusting God releases the Holy Spirit to bring peace to your heart and take you through what is challenging your peace. In Isaiah 43:2, God beautifully illustrates this,

> 'When you pass through the waters, I will be with you; and when you pass through the rivers, they will not sweep over you. When you walk through the fire, you will not be burned; the flames will not set you ablaze.' (NIV)

Trust God. Allow God to be in control. This allows your heart to be fed by God's promise in Psalm 33:11: *But the plans of the LORD stand firm forever, the purposes of His heart through all generations.* (NIV)

The following three paths to peace will allow God to bring peace to your heart: 1) Live a life trusting God, so that His work in you strengthens your heart. 2) Do not allow sin to linger but allow God to consume any sin that is robbing you of peace. 3) Allow your heart to be formed by God's promises and truths. These three areas will better position your heart to live in peace.

EXPERIENCING CHRIST

Live to know and experience Christ! So many Christians live their Christian lives with a second-hand faith. Their walk with Christ hangs on what God has taught others, not what He has taught them. Their personal time with God often relies more on what others are writing about God rather than what the Word of God is speaking to them. Their disciplines in the faith are done without the expectation of being touched by God, but merely performing a duty. They live life being indifferent to what God's Word says. Living apathetically results in a heart that is incrementally being made numb to God. A heart that is numb to God consciously or unconsciously begins to believe and act like there is no God. **You were saved to have a healthy heart that is constantly experiencing the living Christ.**

In Ephesians 3:16-19, you can hear Paul exhorting the Ephesians to pursue Christ in order to experience Him:

I pray that out of His glorious riches He may strengthen you with power through His Spirit in your inner being, so that Christ may dwell in your hearts through faith. And I pray that you, being rooted and established in love, may have power, together with all the saints, to grasp how wide and long and high and deep is the love of Christ, and to know this love that surpasses knowledge — that you may be filled to the measure of all the fullness of God. (NIV)

Paul admonishes you to experience Christ in such a way that your heart is overflowing with Jesus. **God did not save you to experience the Christian life with a secondhand faith, but through the overwhelming and overflowing work of the Holy Spirit in you.**

Many Christians do not have the heart to go through the eye of the needle because they are not experiencing Christ. Their hearts are gaunt with hunger for experiencing Jesus. You can move from malnutrition to fullness by responding to God's promptings in your heart as you do your spiritual disciplines while walking faithfully with God each day. Every time you respond to God by stepping out in faith, you release more of the work of Christ in your heart. This active faith results in an ever-increasing experience of God's work and love. The opposite of this is practicing spiritual disciplines with no anticipation of Christ speaking and acting. Jesus is in your heart, but your lack of faith and conviction makes Him no part of your life. Before doing any spiritual discipline, ask the Holy Spirit to speak to your heart and reveal the truths in Scripture. Luke 24:45 confirms this: *Then He opened their minds so they could understand the Scriptures. (NIV)*

A friend of mine shared how God blessed him with a great truck at an unbelievable price. In the course of doing business, he found a truck for sale at one of his customers. He had been praying for such a vehicle. Upon inquiring about the price, the man said he would sell it for $4,000 to $5,000. My friend thought this was a great price. His due diligence suggested the truck was probably worth $10,000. This truck would be an incredible blessing at $5,000, except he felt he would be taking advantage of the gentleman. He called him and told him he wanted to buy his truck, and asked "What would the price be?" The gentleman said $5,000. Human nature would say take the great deal as God's blessing, but my friend's conscience said that he should first look to the other's best interest. My friend explained to the man what his research found, and that he would be giving away $5,000. The man said that was okay. He did not drive it anymore and the truck was in the way by sitting in his driveway. Whether the man raised the price or gave the great deal, God was honored. In this case my friend was blessed with the truck, **but his actions pointed to Jesus because his focus was to be faithful to God and His truths rather than save some money.** Next time my friend is confronted with God's way or the world's ways, his heart will pump more strongly in anticipation of how he will experience more of God.

The experience of seeing God at work is far more valuable than the temporal benefit of a worldly gain. Stepping by faith into an experience that is less than clear on the result allows you to be filled and controlled by the Holy Spirit instead of the crafty ways of human nature. Experiencing more of Jesus will result in more of Him being in your heart. Oh, how Paul wanted Christians to experience Jesus! Paul's heart revealed more of the power of experiencing Jesus in Colossians 1:10-12:

> *And we pray this in order that you may live a life worthy of the Lord and may please Him in every way: bearing fruit in every good work, growing in the knowledge of God, being strengthened with all power according to His glorious might so that you may have great endurance and patience, and joyfully giving thanks to the Father, who has qualified you to share in the inheritance of the saints in the kingdom of light. (NIV)*

God wants you to personally experience the living Christ. Pursue Jesus as never before so that your heart may be unwavering from experiencing more of God.

FEEDING THE HEART

What is the food of your life? How might you answer this question in past tense on your death bed? A possible Christian answer would be "Every Word that comes from the Bible." God's spoken Word in the Bible would certainly appear correct. In John 6:35 Jesus answered this question in this way: *Jesus declared, "I am the bread of life. He who comes to Me will never go hungry, and he who believes in Me will never be thirsty.* (NIV) This verse was spoken to an unbeliever, but it also speaks to Christians. Just as an unbeliever comes to salvation through Christ, so a Christian comes to Christ for fueling his faith. A Christian must constantly feed on Christ to experience the full character and life of Christ. A Christian who seldom draws on Christ will deplete their spiritual tank.

Live your life in Christ in the reality that your days on this earth are fed and refreshed through the life of Jesus in you. Every pulse of your life on this temporal earth should flow out of your relationship with Jesus. This relationship with Jesus will increasingly bring you to the reality that the things of this world do not satisfy; they divert you from the real sustenance of life: Jesus. Instead of your life being consumed by the things of this world, you must find increasing satisfaction through the righteousness of Jesus. Jesus' righteousness is not an adjunct to life, but the very sustenance of life. **Jesus' character is like a well-fitted suit instead of a suit three sizes too small.** Your heart must pound to the righteousness of Jesus knowing that He not only satisfies but is also life itself.

God created the world to give your heart satisfaction through

the prism of His glory. The prism of God's glory is living life under the power and direction of Christ. It is only here that your cravings are satisfied, and false idols become spoiled food. **The union of truth with your heart strengthens your love for righteousness.**

Let's look at the most exploited pleasure of life, sex, as an example of people trying to find satisfaction. Practiced according to God's principles, sexual pleasure takes you deeper into relationship with your spouse. Sex practiced outside of God's principles objectifies, demeans, abuses, and selfishly takes for personal gain. The pleasure of sex can be found in both paths initially, but the world's way ends in destruction, while God's way ends in satisfaction. Likewise, God designed every human being to find real satisfaction through the living Word of God. Satisfaction outside of this would be like trying to hold water in a strainer. A strainer was not meant to hold liquid. The same would be true for anyone seeking satisfaction apart from God's way. The satisfaction they seek would be fleeting and insatiable, while God's satisfaction is gratifying and fulfilling.

A HEART FOR RIGHTEOUSNESS

In Psalm 17:15, David revealed a heart of righteousness: *As for me, I shall behold Thy face in righteousness; I will be satisfied with Thy likeness when I awake.* (*NASB*) David's heart beat for righteousness. He saw the inseparable link between living a righteous life while beholding the face of God. Feel David's passion for experiencing the very presence and personality of God. Not only did he have a passion for it, but he also proclaimed total comfort in living God's way in a sinful and corrupt world. This heart for God and His ways was cultivated through a life pursuing and dwelling with God.

God wants you to have a steadfast heart that wants what He wants. A heart whose satisfaction is found in God alone; a heart that easily diverts from illusory gratifications to experiencing God

Himself; a heart that loves righteousness for the sheer pleasure of being more in God's presence. It is this follower of Christ who finds no greater satisfaction in all of life than beholding the righteousness of God! The heart that beats like this has grasped what true satisfaction is and is ready to go through the eye of the needle. Psalm 34:15 shows God's response to those whose hearts crave righteousness, *The eyes of the LORD are on the righteous and His ears are attentive to their cry. (NIV)*

A HEART FOR GOD

A heart for God is one who has experienced increasing measures of God's love, and out of that love has grown to fear Him. Love for God and fear of God are inseparable. Fearing God is a reverence, awe, and obedience that flows from knowing Him and His love. You know God by experiencing deeper levels of relationship and obedience. Psalm 33:18 shows the companionship of love and fear: *But the eyes of the LORD are on those who fear Him, on those whose hope is in His unfailing love.* (NIV) Psalm 103:11 shows the interdependence of love and fear: *For as high as the heavens are above the earth, so great is His love for those who fear Him.* (NIV) The burgeoning growth of God's love in you will stimulate a greater fear of God as you better understand His love and compassion for you.

You move closer to going through the eye of the needle as your understanding and experience of God illuminates an enlarging view of God's greatness, glory, and love. Your love for and fear of God grow in tandem as they both feed one another. Your love for God allows you to better know Him which leads to a greater fear of Him. This growth develops greater hope through your increasing certainty of God's love and the experience of His faithfulness as you step out in faith. This growth and hope make you feel increasingly peaceful and comfortable living in God's presence. It is this comfort and peace that makes it easier to further trust God with more of the details of your life. Seeing the interdependence of love, fear, hope, and faith gives you a better picture of Hebrews 11:1: F*aith is being sure of what we hope for and certain of what we do not see.* (NIV) You can say love and fear are your launching pad for faith and hope. Your love and knowledge of God breeds a healthy fear that propels steps of obedience out of faith and trust for God.

Love, fear, and faith are essential nutrients for growing a heart for God. As you read this Scripture, you can almost see the satisfied smile on David's face as he wrote Psalm 34:7-8:

The angel of the LORD encamps around those who fear Him, and He delivers them. Taste and see that the LORD is good; blessed is the man who takes refuge in Him. (NIV)

David's relationship with God caused His love, fear, and faith to dramatically grow. This growth fueled his passion to encourage others to taste and see the Lord's goodness, so that they too could experience more of Him. This very thing happened in John 4:28-29 when the woman at the well challenged the town to go experience the living Christ: *Then, leaving her water jar, the woman went back to the town and said to the people, 'Come, see a man who told me everything I ever did. Could this be the Christ?'* (NIV) Let your heart be filled with faith, love, and fear for God, so you too can experience the hope of the living Christ.

A HEART FOR PEOPLE

Psalm 37:28 describes a character trait that is critical for having a heart for God: *For the LORD loves the just and will not forsake His faithful ones.* (NIV) We live in a world that puts "me" first and "you" wherever you happen to land. God loves those who are just. A just heart is other-centered instead of self-centered. Jesus repeatedly taught that we need to put others ahead of self. Two stories in the New Testament capture the hearts of other-centered people. Luke 15:11-24 tells the story of the Prodigal Son. In verse 20, Jesus describes loving someone who has offended you instead of clinging to the offense you experienced from him:

> *'But while he was still a long way off, his father saw him (prodigal son) and was filled with compassion for him; he ran to his son, threw his arms around him and kissed him. (NIV)*

The father's love and sacrifice for this prodigal son had been treated with indifference and disrespect. His son preferred his inheritance over his father. On his son's return after abandoning his father, the father put his son's change of heart first instead of the offenses he had suffered. Our old nature thinks quite differently: "Here is my son who ignored all my teachings growing up; who abandoned what I worked so hard for him to have; who squandered the inheritance I gave him; and now he returns for more." Our old nature also responds quite differently by saying, "I was right and you were wrong; you have no stature here after what you did; look at your brother, who was responsible and faithful; you handled yourself so poorly, you do not deserve anything." None of these statements would be undeserved, but **malice does not change the heart, only love changes the heart.** The father accepted the son back unconditionally. He loved him regardless of what he had done. The father exhibited a just character by providing fertile ground for God to change his son's heart.

In Jesus' parable of the Good Samaritan in Luke 10:30-35, we see how the character of a just man puts the interest of another above his own:

'A man was going down from Jerusalem to Jericho, when he was attacked by robbers. They stripped him of his clothes, beat him and went away, leaving him half dead. A priest happened to be going down the same road, and when he saw the man, he passed by on the other side. So too, a Levite, when he came to the place and saw him, passed by on the other side. But a Samaritan, as he traveled, came where the man was; and when he saw him, he took pity on him. He went to him and bandaged his wounds, pouring on oil and wine. Then he put the man on his own donkey, took him to an inn and took care of him. The next day he took out two silver coins and gave them to the innkeeper. "Look after him," he said, "and when I return, I will reimburse you for any extra expense you may have."' (NIV)

The first two travelers, despite being religious, did not have hearts of compassion to care for this man in need. The Samaritan, who was despised by the religious, stopped and helped the wounded man. The Samaritan was not deterred by the potential of danger, loss of time, and the cost of caring for this man. To assure the man's full recovery, he went the extra mile by being willing to incur added cost and time on his return to be certain the wounded man was treated well. The Samaritan exhibited a just character by caring for and being faithful to the injured stranger. The Samaritan most likely had excuses similar to the first two travelers, but he had a heart for people.

Being other-centered is not one of many commands, but one of two commands given in Matthew 22:37-40 on which all the other laws are based:

Jesus replied: '"Love the Lord your God with all your heart and with all your soul and with all your mind." This is the first and greatest commandment. And the second is like it: "Love your neighbor as yourself." All the Law and the Prophets hang on these two commandments.' (NIV)

The essence of God is love. Love represents itself best in caring for the interests of others above your own interests. A just heart wants what is best for the other person. The previous two Bible stories are great examples of this. Here are six broad principles for living a just life that cares for and loves others.

- 1 Corinthians 10:32-33: *Do not cause anyone to stumble, whether Jews, Greeks, or the church of God — even as I try to please everybody in every way. For I am not seeking my own good but the good of many, so that they may be saved.* (NIV) Live a life that seeks the good of others before your own good. Your treatment of and relationship with another should place his needs first, then your own. This selfless lifestyle positions unbelievers for salvation.
- 1 Corinthians 9:22: *I have become all things to all men so that by all possible means I might save some.* (NIV) Be willing to adapt and adjust while not violating God's truths. This makes it easy for others to enjoy who you are as a Christian while minimizing any potential barriers. You may disagree with the beliefs and actions of another, but finding the proper interaction, interest, and support causes others to see Christ rather than a self-absorbed person.
- 1 Corinthians 13:5 Speaks of love: *It is not rude, it is not self-seeking, it is not easily angered, <u>it keeps no record of wrongs.</u>* (NIV) This passage has many great attributes for loving others, but keeping no record of wrongs is especially important in loving others. Tracking wrongs is rooted in being judgmental. It is difficult for a relationship to be clothed in love if you are continually feeding a judgmental attitude

against the other. **A heart of love unconditionally embraces the other, so that God's love is not diverted by the tracking of past actions.** God uses this kind of lifestyle to channel His unconditional love.

- Philippians 2:4-5: *Each of you should look not only to your own interests, but also to the interests of others. Your attitude should be the same as that of Christ Jesus.* (NIV) Live so others' interests are placed above yours. Your interests should not be for your gain, but for the gain of others.
- Romans 15:2: *Each of us should please his neighbor for his good, to build him up.* (NIV) Live to build up others, not to tear them down. Love adds to relationships, while sin diminishes them. Look for the hearts of others so that you can see how to build them up.
- 1 Corinthians 8:9: *Be careful, however, that the exercise of your freedom does not become a stumbling block to the weak.* (NIV) Do not say, practice, or partake of anything that changes the discussion from Jesus to how you live. Do not assume what God has taught or done in your life is necessarily beneficial to others. Christ's love in you should encourage and grow others instead of confuse and tear down. **As the story that God has crafted in your life has taken time, it may take time to help others enter into their story with God through salvation or growth in their Christian walk.**

God has called Christians to be selfless; in this way, they can be vessels for His use. You begin to block God's presence and work in others when you start adding your agenda, needs, habits, and priorities. The first commandment in Matthew 22:37 is to *Love the Lord your God with all your heart.* (NIV) Loving God first begins the process of living a just life that puts others first and yourself second. Philippians 2:6-8 shows this selflessness in Jesus:

Who, being in very nature God, did not consider equality with God something to be grasped, but made Himself nothing, taking the very nature of a servant, being made in human likeness. And being found in appearance as a man, He humbled Himself and became obedient to death — even death on a cross! (NIV)

How much more should you be able to love others after seeing what Jesus did on the cross for you? If Jesus could love you when you were dead in your sins and totally undeserving, you certainly can love others despite what are most generally trivial things that stand in the way. It was God's grace that convicted you of your sin and filled you with His love and hope. It is God's grace that continues to work in you to give you the power and strength to love others, so that God is glorified. **Let the love of Jesus that touched you first be the same love that touches others through your life!**

JESUS' HEART

Who or what has your heart? The owner of your heart is in control of your life. You may speak Jesus, act Godly, and proclaim His mission, but if you own your heart, those proclamations of Christ are only vapors in your vast world of idols. In Galatians 2:20 Paul identifies Jesus' ownership:

I have been crucified with Christ and I no longer live, but Christ lives in me. The life I live in the body, I live by faith in the Son of God, who loved me and gave Himself for me. (NIV)

The ultimate path of your life will be determined by who owns your heart. Giving Christ ownership of your heart sets you up for going through the eye of the needle. **The victorious Christian life is not a product of your will and actions, but the submission of your life (heart) to Christ.**

The world, the strengths of your flesh, and the temptations of satan are formidable foes to Christ owning your heart. We would like to think that having Jesus in our hearts removes us from the struggles of life, but not even Jesus was spared hardship and temptations. Right after Jesus was baptized and filled with the Holy Spirit, he was tempted three times In Matthew 4:1-11. Most Christians are familiar with these temptations but may not have placed them in everyday life settings. As you read these three temptations, let them relate to your real-life temptations.

- After 40 days and nights of fasting the devil said, in verse 3-4: *'If You are the Son of God, tell these stones to become bread.' Jesus answered, 'It is written: "Man does not live on bread alone, but on every word that comes from the mouth of God."'* (NIV) When life wears you down to the nub, you too will be tempted. Will you continue to trust God, or will you take things into your own hands? Will the bare needs of your life remove God from the throne, or will you continue to believe and stand on God's Word?
- Then the devil appealed to the vanity of man in verses 6-7: *'If you are the Son of God,'* he said, *'throw yourself down.' Jesus answered him, 'It is also written: "Do not put the Lord your God to the test."'* (NIV) Being Godly, doing what is right, and putting others first does not elevate you in the eyes of the world, but it does with God. This temptation dares you to show everyone who you are and of what you are made. Proving your self-worth can be irresistible, unless your heart says, "I am going to trust and serve God alone."
- Finally, the devil tempted Jesus with power and wealth in verses 8-10: *Again, the devil took Him to a very high*

mountain and showed Him all the kingdoms of the world and their splendor. 'All this I will give You,' he said, 'if You will bow down and worship me.' Jesus said to him, 'Away from Me, satan! For it is written: "Worship the Lord your God, and serve Him only."' (NIV) Our world is obsessed with wealth, power, and things. It seems like you can never get enough. What used to satisfy you now calls for ownership of you. The lifestyle you once dreamed of having now makes you yearn for many more things. After your tenth increase in income you can hear yourself saying, "With just a little more income all my needs can be covered." Will Jesus remain in charge when you are tempted to get things you have always wanted and desired, or will you say, like Jesus, "I worship and serve Him (God) only."

Allowing Jesus to maintain ownership of your heart will be a daily struggle, but continuing to crucify your flesh at the cross will bring increasing success. Paul explains it this way in 2 Corinthians 4:11: *For we who are alive are always being given over to death for Jesus' sake, so that His life may be revealed in our mortal body.* (NIV)

Having a heart for God is not only a daily quest, but also a daily transformation. Living in each of these eight areas will open your life to God, killing the old self in order that your new heart can live.

SEVEN

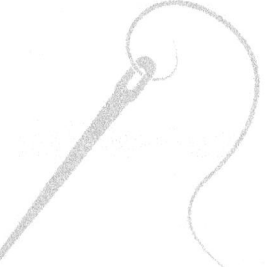

Having the Will to Go Through the Eye of the Needle

YOUR HEART CAN BE READY to go through the eye of the needle, but do you have the will to go through the eye of the needle? Your heart represents God's work and change in you, while your will represents your willingness to respond to your heart's leadings. Your changed heart causes you to desire, want and believe God's truths; but you may lack the faith to embrace them. You are comfortable speaking about the changes God is producing in you, but your faith is not there to act on your beliefs. You lack the will.

The rich man who approached Jesus about salvation appeared to have a heart for God, but he was not sold out to God. He did not have the will to embrace God, His purposes, or His way. Your heart is of great value, but the will to step forward and act is crucial. Your heart can be idealistic while the will to act offers finality. So many Christians live in a Christian utopia, espousing Christian virtues and ideals while never acting upon them. It is great to say you love your neighbor, but how many times a day are we confronted with opportunities to love, help, and minister in practical ways to others? Serving such as mowing the lawn for an elderly person; serving food to someone in distress; caring for someone's kids who are at their wits end; or listening to a troubled person seeking help. For many Christians, their faith in Christ is expressed disproportionately in moral platitudes instead of action.

Two of the main characters on the TV show Scorpion bring this to life. Walter O'Brian, the main character who has an IQ of 197, is used by the government to save the country from catastrophe time and time again. Walter is attracted to his co-star Paige as well as she to him, but neither can vocalize their feelings. In practically every episode, a spark of love and affection is ignited, but it is always quenched. It is almost agonizing to watch, because you know they both want a relationship with each other yet lack the will to make it happen. I wonder if it is just as agonizing for God to watch His children who have been followers of Christ for five, 10, 20, or 40 years still reflect little of His life and purpose? They have inundated their lives with sermons, Bible studies, Christian music, and all types of Christian activities, yet their lifestyles are controlled by areas that reside in the kingdom of this world rather than the kingdom of God. Their ministry to others is a small footnote in their lives.

Do you have the will to go where God desires you to go? Can you imagine God bringing ministry opportunity after ministry opportunity to you, but you ignore them because you do not have the will or the desire to do them? How often does God bring conviction to your life in areas divergent from His ways, but you refuse to let go? How often does God orchestrate your life for His purposes, but you pick your orchestration of life over His? On the inside God is changing your heart to give you the desire for His ways, but your will is focused on the trapping of this world. On the inside and outside, your heart is sold out to God; but you do not have the will to step into God's heart. Gaining the will to obey will help you be made new in the attitude of your mind. There are five elements that can help shape your will and help you respond obediently to God's work within you. Embracing these elements will embolden you for going through the eye of the needle.

WITHIN WHOSE KINGDOM DO YOU RESIDE?

Jesus, facing Pilate, had the opportunity to state His case against being put to death. Jesus could have given a stinging rebuttal for His arrest by the Pharisees. He could have outlined the wonderful things He had done on earth, even how He encouraged responsibility to the Roman Empire. He could have explained how His teachings benefited the Roman Empire. Instead, Jesus answered Pilate in John 18:36 by telling Pilate to Whom He submitted to: *'My kingdom is not of this world...'* (NIV) Jesus was not doing anything to fend for His life. Jesus' greater concern might actually have been for Pilate's soul. Jesus appeared to be pricking Pilot's heart by displaying His peace and assurance as He demonstrated His faith in God. Jesus' clarity of where His life resided obviously touched Pilate by his comments in John 18:38: *'What is truth?'* 19:8: *When Pilate heard this, he was even more afraid.* 19:9: *'Where do you come from?'* 19:12: *Pilate tried to set Jesus free.* (NIV) Pilate knew there was something to fear about Jesus. Without pleading His case, God used Jesus' faithfulness to touch Pilate's life as well as the hearts of others. Jesus was able to do this because He clearly knew where His kingdom resided.

Jesus had a heart for God, and He had the will to follow His heavenly Father, because Jesus knew where He would reside. Living out your life being torn between God and the world is a devolving funnel to total impotency in your Christian life. In Luke 16:10 Jesus tells why,

> *'Whoever can be trusted with very little can also be trusted with much, and whoever is dishonest with very little will also be dishonest with much.'* (NIV)

Sin is a cancer that always grows or continually reoccurs unless you deal with it. Alternating living for God and living for the world only feeds the cancer of sin. Spending time equivocating, justifying, and rationalizing your ways paralyzes the work of the Holy Spirit in you. Living out your life partially in Christ with one foot on earth takes you down a devolving path. You miss the fruit of the Spirit that comes from living in the Kingdom of God. Your walk with Christ increasingly becomes unsatisfying, mystifying, and confusing. This lifestyle causes you to further default to the ways of the world. On the other hand, if you know and affirm that your kingdom is not of this world, it makes it easier for you to choose God's way. Living out of God's kingdom provides a richness of life that stimulates greater devotion to Him. Instead of devolving down to the ways of the world, you ascend to the way of God. As living in God's kingdom becomes more natural and frequent, you will develop a greater love for God and His righteousness.

Recognizing an ambivalent walk with Christ should be a call to measure all your life in terms of living in God's kingdom instead of the world. Ask God to show you your equivocations and compromises. Confess them to God and ask Him to replace them with His way and desires. Let go of this world. Fully embrace the kingdom of God. You will find that the things of this world are enshrouded in sin patterns, habits, and temptations that can quickly consume your will to follow God. As you embrace Jesus as your Source of life, these sin patterns will give way to the work of the Holy Spirit. As this happens, you will gain an increasing will to see your home not of this world, but of the kingdom of God. 1 Timothy 4:16 instructs you in this process:

Pay close attention to yourself and to your teaching; persevere in these things; for as you do this you will insure salvation both for yourself and for those who hear you. (NASB)

Be aware of these areas of dual citizenship so that you can submit them to God and experience His fullness of life. Experiencing more of God's fullness of life will draw you to more of His ways. Remember that areas of dual citizenship arise out of a lack of intimacy in Christ. Walking deeply and passionately with Christ takes you deep into the heart of God giving you greater understanding and wisdom. Paul describes this process in Colossians 1:9-12:

For this reason, since the day we heard about you, we have not stopped praying for you and asking God to <u>fill you with the knowledge of His will</u> through all <u>spiritual wisdom and understanding</u>. And we pray this in order that you may live a life worthy of the Lord and may please Him in every way: <u>bearing fruit in every good work</u>, <u>growing in the knowledge</u> of God, being strengthened with all power according to His glorious might so that you may have great endurance and patience, and joyfully giving thanks to the Father, who has <u>qualified you to share in the inheritance of the saints in the kingdom of light.</u> (NIV)

Notice in this passage how every step of faithfulness feeds further steps of faithfulness. This does not happen when you live with one foot in and one foot out. God's fullness is perfectly revealed and experienced as you make His kingdom your kingdom. Jesus desires every experience with Him to be a deepening of your relationship with Him as well as a growing faith. Jesus abhorred a divided heart. Jesus knew it polluted the will to live for God. Jesus taught this imperative in Matthew 6:24,'*No one can serve two masters. Either* he will hate the one and love the other, or he will be devoted to the one and despise the other.' (NIV) Jesus loves you and desires your continual devotion. **Jesus does not want to be a scheduled activity, but the love of your life. Jesus desires for you to take up full-time residence in His kingdom, not an occasional visitor.** As you consider the beauty of making your kingdom God's kingdom, see how David's life was affected by his decision to fully embrace God in Psalm 63:1-5:

> *O God, you are my God, earnestly I seek You; my soul thirsts for You, my body longs for You, in a dry and weary land where there is no water. I have seen You in the sanctuary and beheld Your power and Your glory. Because Your love is better than life, my lips will glorify You. I will praise You as long as I live, and in Your name I will lift up my hands. My soul will be satisfied as with the richest of foods; with singing lips my mouth will praise You. (NIV)*

Embracing the kingdom of God as your home seems scary. You have spent a lifetime acquiring possessions, gaining position, developing relationships, and creating security. Are you willing to risk it all for the kingdom of God? This decision should be more of an event than a gradual journey. In John 12:24-25, Jesus explains how to do it,

> *'Truly, truly, I say to you, unless a grain of wheat falls into the earth and dies, it remains by itself alone; but if it dies, it bears much fruit. He who loves his life loses it; and he who hates his life in this world shall keep it to life eternal.' (NASB)*

It is only by dying to self that God will truly flourish in you. Put everything in your life on God's altar for Him to have and use. Give God the keys to your house, car, memberships, clubs, and whatever else controls your life. It is only by allowing God to be Lord of your life that you will bear and experience the fruit He has for you.

LOVING RIGHTEOUSNESS

Righteousness is critical for having the will to go through the eye of the needle. It is not so much about doing righteous things, but about your character and identity exuding righteousness. Our tendency is to correlate righteousness with acts as opposed to a righteous nature driving your actions.

Not long ago I went to Sam's Club to return something. (Now we are getting into true confessions!) I love Drumstick ice cream cones. That is Love with a capital L. For those of you who have not been introduced to this ecstasy, it is vanilla ice cream (great ice cream), put in a cone (delicious cone), covered with chocolate (rich, sweet, delicious chocolate) with a generous covering of peanuts. I bought a box of 16 a small amount, but what do you expect from a man with such self-control? As I ate my way through the box, each and every cone did not have peanuts on it. Exerting great understanding and confidence in the maker, I kept thinking it was a random error. After the twelfth cone, I had enough of random error. I was going to get a refund for the remaining four cones while praying that they would credit the whole box – knowing the agony I had to endure eating twelve cones without peanuts! I got to the counter and began to sheepishly explain this bold action. The two ladies behind the counter were almost laughing while maintaining their professional composure with all 64 of their teeth showing. It seemed like eternity for the first 30 seconds as they began processing the credit, so I asked if I could prove the problem by opening a cone to show them. Plus, it sounded like a good morning snack since it was already 8:05 am! To my horror, the cone was covered with nuts. I said, "No way!" I opened a second and a third with the same result. By then, I am on my knees offering them a cone on me and suggesting there was no need for the credit. They said absolutely not. If that happened on the first twelve, causing me to be dissatisfied, then they were going to credit me. Now that is service with a smile — 64 teeth, that is!

I am sure you have experienced returning an item where they credit you, but tear you apart every step of the way as they write the credit. You got the credit, yes, but will you ever do business again with someone who treats you like that? This store obviously engrained in their policies and people the desire to not only satisfy the customer, but also please them. I came away from there wanting to increase my business with them, plus I got the full credit and a Drumstick to eat while they wrote the credit!

The process the store used to ingrain its employees with a service attitude is similar to how God sanctifies you to live righteously. Jesus died to free you from the law, not for you to labor over it. God made you righteous when you were saved for eternity, but your old self still resides in your old body with all its habits, temptations, and your old environment. Ideally at salvation your new heart, through the work of the Holy Spirit, began transforming the old to the new through the continual process of sanctification. The real change in sanctification begins to happen when righteousness, as described in Psalm 11:7, becomes innate rather than a laborious act: *For the LORD is righteous; He loves righteousness; the upright will behold His face. (NASB)* You live righteously because you love God. Because you love God, you love what He loves; therefore, you want to live righteously. Loving God, loving righteousness, and living righteously brings you into the constant presence and work of God – metaphorically experiencing the face of God – God Himself.

Beholding the face of God changes the whole dynamic of living righteously. Instead of living righteously because you feel you must or because God wants you to, you live righteously out of your love for God; you desire to please Him and hunger for the joy of experiencing Him through His design. This lifestyle has the will to go through the eye of the needle.

Another change occurs in loving righteousness. You read the Word not out of habit or duty, but because you hunger for more of His righteousness. Proverbs 2:1-4 illustrates this:

> *My son, if you will receive my sayings, and treasure my commandments within you, make your ear attentive to wisdom, incline your heart to understanding; For if you cry for discernment, lift your voice for understanding; If you seek her as silver, and search for her as for hidden treasures; then you will discern the fear of the LORD, and discover the knowledge of God. (NASB)*

This passage reflects a passionate devotion and hunger for the Word of God. It is not enough to receive God's Word; you must treasure it. It is not enough to ask God for discernment; you must cry out for it. It is not enough to seek truth; you must seek truth because it is of inestimable value. It is not enough to just read the Bible, but to read it for wisdom and understanding to effect life itself. It is this fervency and passion for truth in God's Word that allows God to bring you discernment and wisdom, while touching and transforming your life. It is this passionate devotion for seeking God that reflects a will for whatever God has for you. If you want more of God, seek God by consuming His Word while allowing Him to consume your life with His presence and love. The Word and truth is no longer approached with a give or take mentality, but a mentality that is willing to do whatever is required to live in God's righteousness.

In David's final instruction to Solomon in 1 Chronicles 28:9, he stressed willingness,

> *'And you, my son Solomon, acknowledge the God of your father, and serve Him with wholehearted devotion and with a willing mind, for the LORD searches every heart and understands every motive behind the thoughts. If you seek Him, He will be found by you; but if you forsake Him, He will reject you forever.' (NIV)*

David's final instructions were not about managing the kingdom, good governance, and how to lead, but about loving God, loving righteousness, and living righteously. David wanted his son to be all in for God. Do whatever it takes. Follow God where He is leading you and do what He says. Seek God's righteousness with all your heart, and He will be there with you. A follower of Christ who is willing to do this will go through the eye of the needle.

GOD'S WAY

The main obstacle preventing going through the eye of the needle is the love Christians have for their ways rather than God's way. In Luke 9:57-62, Jesus gives three extreme examples for choosing God over self:

> *As they were walking along the road, a man said to Him (Jesus), 'I will follow You wherever You go.' Jesus replied, 'Foxes have holes and birds of the air have nests, but the Son of Man has no place to lay His head.' He said to another man, 'Follow Me.' But the man replied, 'Lord, first let me go and bury my father.' Jesus said to him, 'Let the dead bury their own dead, but you go and proclaim the kingdom of God.'*

Still another said, 'I will follow You, Lord; but first let me go back and say good-by to my family.' Jesus replied, 'No one who puts his hand to the plow and looks back is fit for service in the kingdom of God.' (NIV)

THE THREE IMPERATIVES FROM LUKE 9:57-62 FOR FOLLOWING JESUS ARE:
1. Choose God over the things in your life.
2. Make God your number one priority while prioritizing everything else around Him.
3. Put God ahead of relationships.

Jesus used these three examples that require great sacrifice causing each person to truly examine his desire and commitment to follow Him. Their hearts were saying yes, but did they have the will to make sacrifices? These three areas challenge any person desiring to follow Jesus to ask, "To whom does my real allegiance belong?" Jesus gave these extreme imperatives to drive away halfhearted followers. The beauty of the Christian life is beholding Christ alive and active in you. The transformative process that Jesus brings is dependent on you whole-heartedly giving your life to Jesus. God, in Revelations 3:15-18 explains:

'I know your deeds, that you are neither cold nor hot. I wish you were either one or the other! So, because you are lukewarm — neither hot nor cold — I am about to spit you out of My mouth. You say, "I am rich; I have acquired wealth and do not need a thing." But you do not realize that you are wretched, pitiful, poor, blind and naked. I counsel you to buy from Me gold refined in the fire, so you can become rich; and white clothes to wear, so you can cover your shameful nakedness; and salve to put on your eyes, so you can see.' (NIV)

Your deeds pollute God's ability to produce abundant life in you. Instead of being a growing, flourishing child of God, you have become a Christian mired in the ravages of carnal living. God's best shot of transformation is a sold-out life that is fully devoted to His way.

In the comfort of your home, surrounded by friends, and with many options on what to do with your life, it is easy to see the Christian life as a nice add-on to your routine. Jesus wants each person's commitment to be a true, unwavering commitment that has already counted the costs and is ready to make Him Lord. King David's wife loved being queen, but treasured David's position as king more than glorifying God. 2 Samuel 6:21b-22a tells how David treasured God more than the stature of his office when he replied to his wife's denunciation of him, *'I will celebrate before the LORD. I will become even more undignified than this, and I will be humiliated in my own eyes.'* (NIV) In the same way, God wants you, as a follower of Christ, to be willing to bear the costs of discipleship regardless of the outcomes. Glorifying God means your life is ordered around Him first. Are you willing to choose God first when you are faced with personal sacrifice for the kingdom of God? Choosing Jesus over the world demonstrates your trust in Him and allegiance to Him being first. Trusting Jesus means you relinquish control to Him. This removes what you saw as obstacles, because those obstacles now belong to God and are under His control. Paul described how this lifestyle looks in 2 Corinthians 5:15: *And He died for all, that those who live should no longer live for themselves but for Him who died for them and was raised again.* (NIV) Having the will to live for Christ, not yourself, positions you to go through the eye of the needle.

DIVINE OR HUMAN?

Trusting God requires a changed mindset. So many people say they believe in God, but do they really? The way you trust God ultimately affirms your beliefs about Him and who He is. Some people believe God offers moral insights and direction. Others believe they should live their lives to their best ability knowing God will be pleased with their efforts. Both these mindsets have some truth, but 2 Peter 1:3 stresses God's role in meeting our needs:

His divine power has given us everything we need for life and Godliness through our knowledge of Him who called us by His own glory and goodness. (NIV)

God is not only there, but He is also divinely and intimately working in each Christian's life. God's work in you is only restricted by your faith in Him. There is a mutual connection between faith and trust that says your trust in God ends where your faith ends. In other words, little faith will produce little trust and great faith will cause you to trust God expansively. One time I was in a restaurant eating when I saw a person pummeling another person outside with a large glass bottle. There was another man looking on. My belief is it is safest for me not to interfere in any altercation, but as I watched, I did not feel right just letting this happen. I felt God calling me to intervene. Mentally, I knew I should not intervene for my safety, not knowing what the aggressor or onlooker possessed, but spiritually I felt God telling me to do it. Fortunately, the beating immediately stopped when I intervened. This situation ended well, but even if it had not, I felt God called me to act. I had a peace knowing that I was in God's hands. God does not call us to live our lives with predictability, but rather, as Hebrews 11:6 says, by believing there is a God:

And without faith it is impossible to please God, for whoever would approach Him must believe that He exists and that He rewards those who seek Him. (NRSV)

God wants you to live your life in Christ trusting His divine power rather than your human power. Every step and turn in life will bring you to this intersection of faith and trust. Satan says your God is not going to come through. The world says to live this way because everyone does it and the benefits are great. Self says, "I do not want to alienate those who I care about or are counting on me." Everything screams to take the worldly road instead of the divine road. In Esther 4:16 we see how Esther handled a life-and-death predicament by choosing the divine path:

'Go, gather together all the Jews who are in Susa, and fast for me. Do not eat or drink for three days, night or day. I and my maids will fast as you do. When this is done, I will go to the king, even though it is against the law. And if I perish, I perish.' (NIV)

Despite the danger, she trusted God with the results. She knew that whatever she humanly could do would fall short of what God's power could do. Ultimately, you must have the will to plug into God's divine power. This comes from immersing yourself in Jesus so that you can grow in intimacy with Him. Problems will draw you to self-solutions, but do you have the will to unconditionally trust God?

The Bible is full of stories of God's people, through faith, trusting God rather than themselves. Daniel 6:7-12 describes how Daniel refused to obey King Darius' decree to pray only to the king. Daniel remained faithful to God, which resulted in him surviving the night in the lion's den. It also caused King Darius to issue a new decree honoring the living God in Daniel 6:26-27,

> *'I issue a decree that in every part of my kingdom people must fear and reverence the God of Daniel. For He is the living God and He endures forever; His kingdom will not be destroyed, His dominion will never end. He rescues and He saves; He performs signs and wonders in the heavens and on the earth. He has rescued Daniel from the power of the lions.' (NIV)*

If Daniel had used all his human prowess, he still would not have survived the lion's den. But Daniel had the faith to trust God, which resulted in King Darius and many people in the kingdom honoring and revering God. God's name and glory were proclaimed throughout the kingdom.

Another example is the courage Silas and Paul showed in prison in Acts 16:16-34. They demonstrated their boldness by praying and singing hymns to God as well as putting others' interests ahead of their own. When God opened the jail doors by an earthquake, Paul and Silas could have fled for safety. But they stayed to assure the safety of the jailer. In Acts 16:33-34 you see how their actions resulted in the jailer and his family's salvation:

> *At that hour of the night the jailer took them (Paul and Silas) and washed their wounds; then immediately he and all his family were baptized. The jailer brought them into his house and set a meal before them; he was filled with joy because he had come to believe in God — he and his whole family. (NIV)*

Trusting in your divine God, and not your human capabilities allows you to plug into God's divine power and providence. This kind of trust fully immerses you into God, allowing Him to fully release His power and work in you. As you see in the lives of Esther, Daniel, Paul, and Silas, **life may not be easy. Philippians 2:12 says**

it is when your and God's wills connect, you experience God Himself:

Therefore, my dear friends, as you have always obeyed — not only in my presence, but now much more in my absence — continue to work out your salvation with fear and trembling. (NIV)

Paul goes on to write in Philippians 2:13 that it is your life of trusting Christ that allows God's best in you: *For it is God who works in you to will and to act according to His good purpose.* (NIV) You trust God no matter the size of the wave coming at you, because you know He is working for your good as well as the good of those around you. Habakkuk 3:17-18 is an illuminating Scripture on trusting God:

Though the fig tree does not bud and there are no grapes on the vines, though the olive crop fails and the fields produce no food, though there are no sheep in the pen and no cattle in the stalls, yet I will rejoice in the LORD, I will be joyful in God my Savior. (NIV)

This passage describes praising God no matter the circumstances. You cannot trust God only when your barns are filled with plenty; you can trust Him all the time. It is during difficultly that trusting God illuminates your faith. There were twelve disciples passing out bread and fish to the 5,000 (probably 10,000 including wives and children) in Matthew 14:16-21. Would you have taken your portion of the five loaves and two fish to pass out to the crowd, or would you have volunteered for another job? Does your faith only exert itself when it is easy and predictable? "Easy task, so I will trust God, but ask me to feed 5,000 with almost half a loaf of bread and a sixth of a fish, I think I will figure out another way to feed this crowd." **Life without the will to exercise your faith in the divine is starving your spiritual body.** Every denial of faith by not trusting Him makes your God that much smaller. No grapes on the vine, no food in the field, my stalls are empty of cattle and sheep, and I am hungry, But I will rejoice in God, because I know my God and have the faith to trust Him in the most destitute of circumstances!

Your faith will ultimately reflect your will to go through the eye of the needle. Listen to Paul describe his faith and will as he prays in Ephesians 1:19-20:

> *I pray also that the eyes of your heart may be enlightened in order that you may know the hope to which He has called you, the riches of his glorious inheritance in the saints, and His incomparably great power for us who believe. That power is like the working of His mighty strength, which He exerted in Christ when He raised Him from the dead and seated Him at His right hand in the heavenly realms. (NIV)*

If God could raise Jesus from the dead, that was good enough for Paul. Paul knew and was reconciled to believing what he wrote in 2 Corinthians 3:5: *Not that we are competent in ourselves to claim anything for ourselves, but our competence comes from God. (NIV)* There was nothing Paul could do, because only Christ, Himself, could carry His message, life, and purpose forward. 2 Corinthians 4:7 says that Paul was merely an instrument in God's hands: *But we have this treasure in jars of clay to show that this all-surpassing power is from God and not from us. (NIV)* **Our treasure is God in us, redeemed by our Savior, filled with the Holy Spirit to walk through every life experience with Him.** God only asks for available hands to use for His purposes. 2 Thessalonians 1:11 describes God working in this type of person:

With this in mind, we constantly pray for you, that our God may count you worthy of His calling, and that by His power He may fulfill every good purpose of yours and every act prompted by your faith. (NIV)

God wants you to experience Him, but are you willing to answer His call?

CHOOSING GOD

Having the will to go through the eye of the needle ultimately boils down to choosing God over anything else that might displace Him. You cannot hold onto sin while going through the eye of the needle! You will either hold onto sin and stay on this side of the eye, or you will let go of sin, trusting God as you take the trip through the needle. Which are you choosing? You will ultimately capitulate to sin or to God. You give in to the temptations of satan because of the attractiveness of his allures, or the world that is filled with endless opportunities for sinning, or your flesh which constantly screams for more satisfaction outside of God. All of these are ultimately a surrender to sin. Satan, the world, and the flesh have a full-time staff of marketers that are playing up the benefits of life away from God, while God has His Truth that is written in the Bible and is testified to by the Holy Spirit. God markets His Truth through the transforming process of intimately knowing Jesus as the Holy Spirit transforms your life to Jesus. Ultimately, this is a battle of immense proportions. Romans 12:21 describes it simply by saying: *Do not be overcome by evil, but overcome evil with good. (NASB)*

The secret for choosing God is having the will to go through the eye of the needle. This sounds easy until Jesus lays out the problem in Matthew 26:41, *'Watch and pray so that you will not fall into temptation. The spirit is willing, but the body is weak.'*

(*NIV*) This sounds like a negative, but it is more of a warning. Just like the body becomes weak from lack of nutrition and food, in the same way your spirit becomes weak from lack of spiritual nutrition. Accepting this as a truth then asks the question, **"Do you have the will to properly nourish your spirit?"** You are in the desert if you are practicing insufficient spiritual disciplines or are you performing the disciplines without responding to God's leadings. Job 23:12 puts a lot of substance to this statement, *'I have not departed from the commands of His lips; I have treasured the words of His mouth more than my daily bread.'* (*NIV*) **Satan, the world, and the flesh will always plague your spirit, but the Holy Spirit thrives in overcoming evil through your healthy spirit.**

The will to choose God above evil becomes easier as your intimacy with Christ makes Him the most important thing in life. The growing depth of your relationship with Christ will challenge every bit of your being to choose God over evil. Your will to obey increases like a snowball rolling down a snow-covered mountain slope. Each roll picks up more snow, making it bigger and easier to roll. In the same way, God's work in you feeds the will to choose Him over anything else. Every time you trust God, your faith increases, making it a little easier to follow and trust Him in the future. **There will be setbacks and trials as your faith grows, but these are opportunities for continued growth and sanctification.**

EIGHT

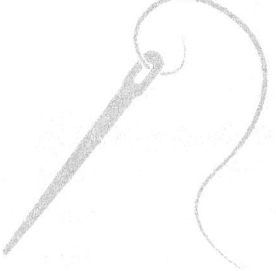

Stepping Through the Eye of the Needle

THE PREVIOUS SEVEN CHAPTERS CULMINATE in this chapter, which is hopefully anticlimactic because you have allowed the previous chapters to open you up to God's work in your life. Each chapter was designed to peel away the veneers of the world that block God. This is like what a massage therapist does by methodically working every muscle throughout the body to free you from your aches and pains. The Holy Spirit acts similarly by opening your life to bad habits, spiritual deficiencies, and spiritual cancers that are sabotaging, if not destroying, your relationship with God. **As you exposed your life to God's truths in the previous chapters, the Holy Spirit was freed to further sanctify your life in Christ. In other words, the Holy Spirit has already begun the process of taking you through the eye of the needle!**

For seven chapters, your spiritual life has been tenderized with

God's Word, truths, and principles. I use the word tenderize to help you become more sensitive to the work the Holy Spirit is already doing in you and to encourage you to allow God to continue working in hardened areas. Prayer, Bible study, and application of God's Word will all facilitate the ongoing transformative process that God is doing in you.

I would like to use the analogy of a funnel to help you understand the concept of going through the eye of the needle. The funnel represents your life. The funnel is filled with things that are blocking God's liberating, transformative, and abundant life in you. You progress through the funnel as the Holy Spirit deals with those things that are hindering or blocking your relationship with God. Liquid pouring through a funnel passes more rapidly as you get closer to the spout. A similar spiritual experience happens as you approach the eye of the needle. In the beginning, you approach with hesitancy or unwillingness to change the areas of growth that have been revealed by the Holy Spirit . The more you obey the Holy Spirit's convictions, the less resistance and hesitancy you will have. Like the funnel, the closer you come to the eye of the needle, your desire for following Christ will accelerate Christ's work in you. You will have a greater and closer experience with Christ and His work as you allow Him to take control of your life. Your heart will be naturally attracted to desiring and experiencing more of God.

A gentleman I was discipling at a homeless shelter shared his anxiety over getting out of the program. He feared the possibility of using drugs again or being coaxed back into sin by old relationships. At some point in your journey to total Lordship, you will probably stop to look through the end of the funnel (the eye of the needle). This is like a final reckoning of your life with Christ. You may even experience anxiety and fear as you consider all that is happening. You may not have come to the point of asking what are the costs, but asking what your life will be like on the other side of the needle? Are you willing to go all the way? Are you still holding back? These are natural responses to the transformative work of the all-consuming Holy Spirit. In Matthew 13:31-32, Jesus reveals the powerful effect of having just a little faith,

> *'The kingdom of heaven is like a mustard seed, which a man took and planted in his field. Though it is the smallest of all your seeds, yet when it grows, it is the largest of garden plants and becomes a tree, so that the birds of the air come and perch in its branches.' (NIV)*

Jesus describes faith as something that grows dramatically when used. Every step of faith allows God to have a stronger grip on your heart which only accelerates your growth and passion for Him.

This chapter's call to action is to obey by believing in God, His promises, and your eternal destiny with Him. Embracing this call to action takes you through the eye of the needle. Even though your steps of faith say you are ready to put everything on the line for God, this still does not make it easy; nor does it tell you what it might look like on the other side.

In 2000 I came to a point in my career where I questioned continuing to work for the company I had been with for 28 years. I held a position that included authority, prestige, good compensation, great benefits, perks, challenges, variety, satisfaction, and enjoyment. But several changes were happening that were stripping away many of the positives, resulting in increasing dissatisfaction. I came to a point where this job no longer seemed like what God wanted in my life. I entered into a time of prayer, extensive Bible reading, Bible study, and listening to God during a time of fasting. I felt God calling me to leave my place of employment, security, and joy of 28 years. I remember looking over the cliff at all I was giving up and not being able to see what was in my future. I was only hearing God say it was time to leave. Not knowing what leaving would look like and having no idea what the future would be brought fear, sadness, and anxiety. I am not certain what my faith looked like at that time, but I believed God had something else for me. God only required my step of faith to trust Him for the future. I did not leave thinking the benefits of my future job would be better, but only that I was in God's hands. I was trusting God for the future and what He desired for me.

What seemed to consume me most in making this change of vocation was that I had to risk losing the things of this world. Was I willing to trust God enough to give up a substantial income, tremendous travel opportunities, great benefits, significant authority, and great flexibility in life? Up to this point in life, my future had been largely scripted by my talents, education, and the safety nets of this world. Was I willing to take this step of faith by being willing to give up all I had and step into a world of uncertainty? In John 12:25, Jesus reveals an important truth for going through the eye of the needle,

> *'I tell you the truth, unless a kernel of wheat falls to the ground and dies, it remains only a single seed. But if it dies, it produces many seeds. The man who loves his life will lose it, while the man who hates his life in this world will keep it for eternal life.' (NIV)*

You must be willing to die to the things that you hold dear as you embrace the kingdom of God. You can make this step of faith through the help of the Holy Spirit, obeying Christ, finding your freedom in Christ, and anchoring to Jesus.

EMPOWERED BY THE HOLY SPIRIT

It is not you, but the Holy Spirit that takes you through the eye of the needle. The amazing thing about God's grace is that He paid the price for your sins as well as provided the means for you to live out your new life in Christ. Jesus explains in John 16:13 the role the Holy Spirit plays in your life,

> 'But when He, the Spirit of truth, comes, He will guide you into all the truth; for He will not speak on His own initiative, but whatever He hears, He will speak; and He will disclose to you what is to come.' (NASB)

The Holy Spirit is always working regardless of your openness or obedience to Him. The first seven chapters were intended to tenderize your life for the work of the Holy Spirit. The process of tenderizing meat can be done by puncturing it with multiple holes, pounding, rolling, heating, or aging it. This makes the meat tender by breaking down any toughness. You can add further flavor by soaking it in a marinade or applying seasonings. In the same way, God has His own tenderization process to open you up to the Holy Spirit working in you.

My prayer is that the Holy Spirit has already begun pounding you, turning up the heat, and poking you, so that He can prod, convict, and guide you into totally yielding to Christ. Hopefully the Holy Spirit has already begun using His Word, uncomfortable experiences, or a trial in your life to reveal your heart towards Him in addition to strengthening your commitment to Christ. 1 Corinthians 2:10 explains how the Holy Spirit reveals what is blocking you, as well as the great things God has for you: *God has revealed it to us by His Spirit. The Spirit searches all things, even the deep things of God. (NIV)* **It is out of the Holy Spirit's convicting, drawing, and empowering that you go through the eye of the needle.**

Jesus, in John 8:31, ties obedience to being a disciple, *'If you hold to My teaching, you are really My disciples.'* (NIV) After making this statement Jesus could have asked, "Are you willing to respond to what I have been saying to you about obeying?" In the same way, you experience God's fullness and abundance by responding in obedience to the Holy Spirit's life and work. Jesus taught in John 8:32, *'Then you will know the truth, and the truth will set you free.'* (NIV) **You will never know the fullness of truth until you wholeheartedly embrace obedience.** God's truth allows you to experience God and His liberating grace that frees you from the slavery of sin, the bondage of the flesh, and the entrapments of this world. Your freedom in Christ frees you to obey, liberates you from fear, and sets you free from anxiety. It is this freedom that takes you through the eye of needle.

LIVING OUT OF THE FRUIT OF RIGHTEOUSNESS

Even though living in freedom can continue to be an ongoing battle, it is a different kind of battle. **Going through the eye of the needle occurs throughout your life, but with increasing ease and greater permanence.** There is something about the first time you take that step of faith. Do you believe in God enough to make this leap of faith? Your faith will be strengthened by every step of faith, but more importantly, you will also taste a little bit of the fruit of righteousness. Experiencing God through the fruit of righteousness begins to radically change the way you approach God as you walk through life. Philippians 1:9-11 describes how your transformation produces the fruit of righteousness:

> *And this is my prayer: that your love may abound more and more in knowledge and depth of insight, so that you may be able to discern what is best and may be pure and blameless*

until the day of Christ, filled with the fruit of righteousness that comes through Jesus Christ — to the glory and praise of God. (NIV)

Every step of faith takes you deeper into God's heart, which results in increasing measures of love, knowledge, insight, and discernment. This transformative growth in Christ manifests itself in purity and blamelessness, which comes from God alone. As God produces this, your life will begin to reveal increasing measures of His character, life, love, and presence. The culminating result of all this is the fruit of righteousness, which starts to put a face on God as you experience more of His power, faithfulness, love, forgiveness, patience, as well as many more of His traits. Your relationship with God will continue to grow and blossom through this reciprocating experience with your infinite Creator.

Even with a vibrant relationship with Christ where you are experiencing His love and work, you will continue to battle temptation and sin in this ungodly world. This does not detract from the power of going through the eye of needle, but points you to the ultimate truth that your life is never beyond the need of God's grace. In John 17:15-19 Jesus speaks of this,

'My prayer is not that You take them out of the world but that You protect them from the evil one. They are not of the world, even as I am not of it. Sanctify them by the truth; Your word is truth. As You sent Me into the world, I have sent them into the world. For them I sanctify Myself, that they too may be truly sanctified.' (NIV)

The world slowly moves from a force that pulls you down to a force that acts as God's tenderizer for breaking down strongholds of sin so that you can be more fully sanctified in Him. Your

increasing sensitivity to sin should drive you into the arms of Jesus … not from Him. Your growing relationship with Jesus and enlarged awareness of the kingdom of God will increasingly make sin less attractive. **Your desire for a closer relationship with Jesus will produce a repulsive taste for anything that might hurt that relationship.** Your expanding reality of who God is will liberate you to live more passionately for Him.

Your burgeoning heart for Jesus and desire to be His hands in this ungodly world will often be confronted with sin. When this happens, do you cloister in the church and attend more Bible studies to protect yourself, or do you do what Paul instructs you to do in 1 Timothy 6:11-12:

> *Flee from these things, you man of God; and pursue righteousness, Godliness, faith, love, perseverance, and gentleness. Fight the good fight of faith; take hold of the eternal life to which you were called, and you made the good confession in the presence of many witnesses. (NASB)*

The Holy Spirit is warning and convicting you of sin as you walk in relationship with Him, so flee from it! The next step is critical: pursue righteousness. **You pursue righteousness by responding to the Holy Spirit's direction!** Go where God is leading you. Godliness, faith, love, perseverance, and gentleness are a natural byproduct of pursuing righteousness. **Pursuing righteousness is good, but perseverance illuminates a Spirit-filled Christian.** The last sentence puts hands and feet for living out your Christian life. Fight with your faith fully in God, in God's way, in the Spirit, and with your eyes on Jesus while believing the promise of eternal life. In all you do, confess the name of Jesus along with how others may know Him. Living your life in this manner puts you in the hands of Jesus. Paul described this walk in Philippians 2:12b-13:

Continue to work out your salvation with fear and trembling, for it is God who works in you to will and to act according to His good purpose. (NIV)

LIVING IN OBEDIENCE

It takes heart, will, and obedience to go through the eye of the needle. We have already explored the importance of having the heart and will, but without obedience, it will not happen. A man I once discipled shared with me how God had put a ministry plan in his heart for his church. Unfortunately, he never wrote it out and presented it. He shared with me the details, which seemed quite good. He had the heart for what God had given him, but he did not have the will to formalize it for presentation, much less the obedience to implement it. Our next meeting was in two weeks, so I said we would postpone the study we were doing and review his plan for the ministry that God gave him. Two weeks later, he presented his ideas for the ministry opportunity. In two weeks he did what he could not in 156 weeks. Now the question was whether he was going to be obedient in working towards implementation. He had reasons why he could not follow through: Young children, too little time, too many other commitments, and a job that required more time than normal. **The difference between comfortable Christianity and costly Christianity is obedience to God.** Unfortunately obedience, more times than not, comes with a cost. For the average Christian, the cost can be offset by adjustments to schedule, spending, and priorities. **The real question is not the time or capability to obey God, but the will and perseverance to obey.**

One of the most talked-about issues in the Bible is obedience. 1 Chronicles 22:13 teaches obedience as well as shows its relationship to success:

You will have success if you are careful to observe the decrees and laws that the LORD gave Moses for Israel. Be strong and courageous. Do not be afraid or discouraged. (NIV)

- You want to go through the eye of the needle: obey.
- You do not have time to obey: make time. Change the problem to an imperative that frees God to use you as His hands and heart in this world.
- You do not have the financial resources to obey: what other financial obligations need to be dropped or changed?
- Your work commitments make it impossible to obey: change your work commitments.
- Your kids' activities do not afford you the time: adjust those activities.

None of these five actions necessarily requires total change, but most will probably require some change. **Some of these realignments may change the way you live, but your obedience will determine God's position in your life.** Is Jesus Lord of your life, or has He been displaced by the idols in your life?

The term, idols, is not frequently used today. It is a great depiction for the things in your life that have gotten in the way of your relationship with God. Be the follower of Christ in 1 Thessalonians 1:9b who serves God before things, people, and activities: *They tell how you turned to God from idols to serve the living and true God. (NIV)* If success comes from simple obedience, do not allow any idol to block an area where God is calling you to obedience. Turn from those idols to the living God. **Pursuing and seeking God is wonderful, but it is out of your obedience that you allow God to work in you.**

ANCHOR TO JESUS

We have come full circle in going through the eye of the needle. The Holy Spirit empowers, directs, and loves you throughout the process of sanctification. As you continue to be transformed through sanctification, the process becomes easier by seeing God's active work in you. Though easier, you can never lose sight that you live in a corrupt world that is always working to take you down. This can be discouraging at times. You can be walking in the center of God's will, yet your relationship with Him can feel desolate. You may feel betrayed by other Christians. Where God is leading you can be difficult as well as painful. Uncertainty and doubt can fill your heart as you look for reassurance and answers. You feel like the Psalmist in Psalm 121:1: *I lift up my eyes to the hills — where does my help come from?* (NIV) Life is supposed to be abundant as you step through the eye of the needle, but you feel lost. Did you miss God? How do you proceed? Hebrews 6:19-20a guides your response:

> *We have this hope as an anchor for the soul, firm and secure. It enters the inner sanctuary behind the curtain, where Jesus, who went before us, has entered on our behalf.* (NIV)

Your anchor is not what the world uses as an anchor; your anchor is in Jesus alone. Jesus went before you and secured your destiny. Yours is not to question, but to stand upon the rock of Christ. You persevere with Jesus as your anchor.

Your journey through life is not about you, but about Jesus. Jesus calls you to obey, while trusting Him for the results. It is not you who makes it happen, but God through His Spirit in you. God's timing always seems to take longer than we think it should. Hold steadfastly to Jesus, your anchor, so that He can take you through the eye of the needle. Hebrews 12:1-2 positions you correctly:

Therefore, since we are surrounded by such a great cloud of witnesses, let us throw off everything that hinders and the sin that so easily entangles, and let us run with perseverance the race marked out for us. Let us fix our eyes on Jesus, the Author and Perfecter of our faith, who for the joy set before Him endured the cross, scorning its shame, and sat down at the right hand of the throne of God. (NIV)

Just as the timing for all the events in Jesus' life was in God's hands, the timing for the events in your life is in His hands. Throw off your doubts and fears and proceed with your eyes firmly on Jesus. **As Jesus authors your journey, He will also perfect it.**

Do not be discouraged if you are tired, weary, and pressed; find your strength and encouragement in Jesus. In my hardest times, I find encouragement and miracles when I replace my hardship, pain, and suffering with the visual image of nails going into Jesus' hands and feet. I see the lashes from the whip ripping flesh from Jesus' body. I quickly come to praise and give thanks for Jesus' suffering and sacrifice for me. I find encouragement in Hebrews 12:3: *Consider Him who endured such opposition from sinful men, so that you will not grow weary and lose heart. (NIV)* I have yet to experience anything in life that comes close to what Jesus endured on the cross for my salvation and sanctification. **I can trust Jesus because He is trustworthy.** I can endure because He gave up so much for me. I can persevere, because Jesus' love and grace will consume my every emotion, feeling, and pain. He is trustworthy and praiseworthy.

The first time I stepped into this visualization, God performed a miracle. I was experiencing extreme pain in both my knees while playing tennis. The pain had grown over the previous weeks, but that day it hit a crescendo. I said, "I have had enough. It is time to have knee surgery." While continuing to play, I began to thank God for my knee pain and how insignificant it was compared to what Christ had done for me. I praised God that the pains I was experiencing on earth were pleasant compared to the suffering Jesus endured. As I continued to play, I thanked God for each burst of pain going through my body as I visualized the extreme pain Jesus experienced on the day of His crucifixion. I felt uplifted and encouraged by the end of the match, but I still had the knee pain. I continued to praise God for the love and grace He showed me through the life and crucifixion of Jesus. Within 48 hours, my knees quit hurting. It has been over twenty years since God healed me. My knees continue to function without pain despite my very active sports program.

Never flinch in going through the needle. Draw upon the Holy Spirit's strength and power. Romans 8:28 tells how the Holy Spirit oversees every detail of our lives: *We know that in all things God works for the good of those who love Him, who have been called according to His purpose. (NIV)* **Look not at what you might be giving up, but instead at all God has done for you.** See the magnificent works Jesus has done and continues to do in your life. Do not allow one work of God's hand in your life go unnoticed and without effect. Obey quickly, because procrastination is satan's tool for confusion. Trust and obey.

Finally, fix your eyes on Jesus, and persevere knowing your future is in His hands. You are along for the ride. Express the same joy, excitement, and perseverance as Paul explained in Philippians 3:10-12:

> *I want to know Christ and the power of His resurrection and the fellowship of sharing in His sufferings, becoming like Him in His death, and so, somehow, to attain to the resurrection from the dead. Not that I have already obtained all this, or have already been made perfect, but I press on to take hold of that for which Christ Jesus took hold of me. (NIV)*

NINE

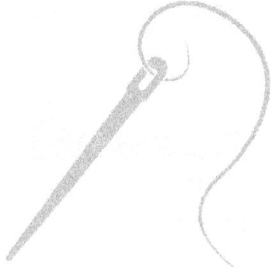

On the Other Side

AS THE CROSS LEADS US to celebrate the resurrection, going through the eye of the needle leads us to celebrate life on the other side. Going through the eye of the needle is like a mother giving birth. Childbirth is painful, but there is no greater joy than holding, kissing, and cuddling your newborn. Life for the mother is now seen through the pristine lens of her newborn's life. Life before and after childbirth are totally different. The exhilaration of your new baby fills you with overwhelming love and joy, but with that comes many new responsibilities, challenges, change of routines, and difficulties. The negatives quickly disappear when seen through the lens of new human life.

Life on the other side of the needle is similar to the entrance of your first child into the family. Nothing is perfect, and life is now seen quite differently. You now view all of life through the Lordship of Christ. You no longer debate theology to determine God's truth, equivocate with what is right and wrong, or live too closely to the things of this world that might tempt or pull you under. Your new heart, enlivened by the Holy Spirit in you, allows the simplicity of the Scripture to speak to you, gives you discernment, and sets you on a path towards righteousness. You no longer straddle life by living between God and the world, because you have made Jesus Lord of your life.

The three-part outline that Ephesians 4:22-24 provided concludes now by putting on the new self:

You were taught, with regard to your former way of life, to put off your old self, which is being corrupted by its deceitful desires; to be made new in the attitude of your minds; and to put on the new self, created to be like God in true righteousness and holiness. (NIV)

You were made righteous when you became a Christian by putting off the old self. You then pursue your life in Christ by being made new in the attitude of your mind so that you can become more like Christ through the process of sanctification. Finally, you put on your new self in righteousness and holiness. This is life on the other side of the needle. You not only put on righteousness, but you also proudly wear it as you live a life in increasing measures of relationship in Christ, righteousness and holiness.

As you continue putting off the old self, being made new in the attitude of your mind, and putting on righteousness, you will see continued transformation into the image of Christ. Areas of compromise needing to be replaced with truth; indifference to God's way will be replaced by a passionate love for Him; a life of divided allegiance will become fully committed to Christ and His way; and temptations will be consumed by your desire for a greater relationship with God. **You will no longer live in the certainty of the things of this world, because you live trusting Him with every aspect of your life. Your life is now fully committed to Christ with no holdbacks. Now your desires and wants are for what God has for you.**

What an incredible position to be in — fully in the hands of Jesus. You are now in the best position to experience the face of God! As you grasp the significance of what God has for you on this side of the needle, please enjoy the magnitude of God's grace. Life on this side may require you to give up some of the things of this world, but you are entering a new area of empowerment and fullness that will far exceed anything you can experience in this world. Allow God's Word and promises to overwhelm your finite expectations with the infinite reality of what God has for you.

YOUR POSITION ON THE OTHER SIDE OF THE NEEDLE

Position is everything on the other side of the needle. Understanding who you are in Christ allows you to embrace and live in your position. In reality you have always had this position but have probably lived life as the Galatians 4:1 Christian I wrote about earlier: *What I am saying is that as long as the heir is a child, he is no different from a slave, although he owns the whole estate.* (NIV) Understanding your position in Christ helps you take hold of it as you enjoy who you are in Christ. Living out who you are in Christ neutralizes so many of the difficulties that Christians experience. Instead of living as an oblivious child, you now live as an heir because of who you are in Christ. You live in the freedom of God's grace and by the power of the Holy Spirit in you!

You must be careful to not hinder taking your position in Christ by continuing in the patterns you developed while living as a slave of the estate. 1 Corinthians 13:11 describes this step of maturity:

When I was a child, I talked like a child, I thought like a child, I reasoned like a child. When I became a man, I put childish ways behind me. (NIV)

Do not just hear, see, and read truths and promises; respond to them! Ask the Holy Spirit to reveal the implications for His truth and how you are to respond. People who have been in bondage tend to come out of bondage slowly because they continue to respond as they did in bondage. The same is true with your new lens of truth. Allow truth to transform you and not just titillate your soul. Your food and drink are no longer the world; your food is your relationship with God, His truth (Word of God), and your life as you live in that truth. Now that God, His truth, and His Word are your meat and drink, you consume truth and respond to it like one who is starving. Your consumption is not out of despair, but sheer delight, because you can experience more of God's grace and love! You will now consume things you used to avoid or not consider because you know the power of releasing more of Christ in you. Who then are you in Christ? Before you know the "who," you must understand your position. Ephesians 2:6-7 describes your position in Christ:

God raised us up with Christ and seated us with Him in the heavenly realms in Christ Jesus, in order that in the coming ages He might show the incomparable riches of His grace, expressed in His kindness to us in Christ Jesus. (NIV)

Knowing, believing, and embracing your position in Christ frees you to live in that position. There is power in the position you now possess. A couple of years ago, my wife and I built a new house. Upon closing, we confidently walked into the mortgage company knowing every detail had been met. We claimed our position at the table because we met the requirements. We were able to close because of our position.

The same is true for a Christian. At salvation, you are not only declared righteous, you are seated with Christ. We have spent eight chapters unpacking the reasons a Christian chooses to be a slave of the world instead of taking his gifted position as an heir to God's kingdom. **Once you unconditionally make Jesus Lord of your life, you strip off the rags you have been wearing and put on the royal clothing of a son of God!** You live out of your position in Christ. In the movie, "Star Wars," Yoda tells Luke, "Use the force." The power is different, but the concept is similar. Just as Yoda told Luke to recognize and embrace the force, so Paul is urging you in Ephesians 1:18-21 to embrace your position in Christ:

> *I pray also that the eyes of your heart may be enlightened in order that you may know the hope to which He has called you, the riches of His glorious inheritance in the saints, and His incomparably great power for us who believe. That power is like the working of His mighty strength, which He exerted in Christ when He raised him from the dead and seated Him at His right hand in the heavenly realms, far above all rule and authority, power and dominion, and every title that can be given, not only in the present age but also in the one to come. (NIV)*

Think of the power you now possess in your position as a child of God, seated with Him in the heavenly realms! Appropriate what God has bestowed on you, by allowing Christ to fully empower you as He further floods your life with His love and grace.

Now for the "who." 1 Peter 2:9 powerfully describes who you are in Christ:

> *But you are a chosen people, a royal priesthood, a holy na-*

tion, a people belonging to God, that you may declare the praises of Him who called you out of darkness into His wonderful light. (NIV)

Not many people on this earth address you with such prestige and importance, yet that is exactly who you are. God did not bring you in as temporary help, but as a royal priest. God bestows on you great privilege in the kingdom of God. This Scripture descriptively details four facets of being a child of God.

First, you are chosen. Chosen is important. Being chosen indicates privilege, purpose and ownership. <u>Privilege</u> because you no longer need a mediator to approach God. Your <u>purpose</u> is loving God and loving people. You love people foremost by sharing the gospel of Christ for their salvation and discipling Christians to better know God as well as to be fruitful. You were also <u>chosen</u> to live as a child of God. As God's child you submit to the Lordship of Christ. You were bought at a price and now live to glorify God in all that you do.

Second, you are a royal priest. You do not have to go through a priest to have access to God because of the sacrifice Jesus made of Himself on the cross. You no longer have to rely upon a mediator because Jesus is your mediator. You are not just a being in human flesh, but a royal priest with all its benefits. You have access to God; you have His life in you; and the Holy Spirit is involved in every detail of your life. As a royal priest, you are to offer up the spiritual sacrifices that are talked about in Hebrews 13:15-16:

Through Jesus, therefore, let us continually offer to God a sacrifice of praise — the fruit of lips that confess His name. And do not forget to do good and to share with others, for with such sacrifices God is pleased. (NIV)

God calls you to serve and minister in His name while praising Him in everything. Your praises and service are a natural response to God's grace and work in you.

Third, you are a holy nation which means you no longer live independently of God. Your very being cries for righteousness. You no longer belong to yourself, others, or organizations; you belong to the one and only living God. As a temple of the Holy Spirit, you give your life as a vessel of righteousness that points to and proclaims God.

Point four is that you are "called into His wonderful light." God owns you and will do anything to protect and care for you. You are called into His marvelous light because your life was not meant to be consumed by the struggles of this world, but to experience and reflect His glorious splendor. Grasp the realities of who you are in Christ and walk in them.

Colossians 1:22 gives your final position in Christ:

But now He has reconciled you by Christ's physical body through death to present you holy in His sight, without blemish and free from accusation. (NIV)

You do not hear much talk from Christians about being blameless today, but you do hear continual talk of being broken, living in a broken world, being sinfully wicked, etc. All are true, but an overemphasis on sin for Christians can have the same effect as an overemphasis on law. Paul describes it in Romans 7:5:

For when we were controlled by the sinful nature, the sinful passions aroused by the law were at work in our bodies, so that we bore fruit for death. (NIV)

Just as you do not continually talk about, point to, and dwell on your lifestyle and mistakes as a child, teenager, or college student, you should not focus on the past as a Christian. As a Christian, you are moving into maturity and focusing on who you are in Christ. Your heart and mind are now centered on your relationship with Christ, God's transforming power, and His continued filling of the Spirit and His work in you.

God has given your past a clean slate so that you are free to live in increasing measures a life without blemish through the Holy Spirit. Mark 10:27 stresses that this possibility is with God alone: *With man this is impossible, but not with God; all things are possible with God.* (NIV) You no longer live life focusing on sin, but God. You do not become consumed with moralism but focus on your relationship with Christ, allowing Him to live His life through you. A man I once discipled had a continual struggle with purity. We studied the Scriptural principles of purity, prayed, put in safeguards, and applied accountability. Nothing seemed to work. I finally told him his problem was that his focus was on purity and not on Jesus. The more he focused on living purely, the more he struggled with purity; when he focused on Jesus, his purity problem disappeared. **Your focus on Jesus grows your relationship with Him while allowing God to change your flesh. Your focus on sin makes it easy for satan to exploit your flesh. Falling more in love with God removes most of the barriers that prevent God's work in you.**

The same is true with marriage. Troubled marriages sometimes get sidetracked with sexual sins. Instead of focusing on growing their marriage, a husband or wife wastes time on sexual immorality. People in problem marriages need to instead focus on better loving and romancing their partners while strengthening their marriages. This will diminish the marital problems, thus removing the temptation for sexual impurity.

Does this mean you can be perfect? No! Does this mean that you are strapped to a treadmill seeking greater perfection? No! **You**

are righteous through the blood of Christ, but you live in an ever-transforming body that is growing to full maturity in Christ. Stepping through the eye of the needle accelerates this process. **Making Christ Lord makes it easier for holiness to spawn more holiness.** As you step by faith into God's kingdom, you experience more of God, grow your relationship with Him, and experience an exhilaration that further strengthens your faith. 1 Thessalonians 5:23-24 describes it this way:

May God Himself, the God of peace, sanctify you through and through. May your whole spirit, soul and body be kept blameless at the coming of our Lord Jesus Christ. The One who calls you is faithful and He will do it. (NIV)

Titus 2:11-12 puts it in layman's terms:

For the grace of God that brings salvation has appeared to all men. It teaches us to say 'No' to ungodliness and worldly passions, and to live self-controlled, upright and godly lives in this present age. (NIV)

If you live in this world, you will struggle with sin. Learn to live life based on your position in Christ, as in Philippians 1:6: *Being confident of this, that He who began a good work in you will carry it on to completion until the day of Christ Jesus.* (NIV)

YOUR LIFE ON THE OTHER SIDE OF THE NEEDLE

Living out your life on the other side of the needle is of utmost importance. Trusting God, deepening your relationship with Christ, loving righteousness, and bearing fruit are four key areas that will illuminate your life in Christ. These four areas reflect the Lordship of Christ rather than living your life in Christ with optional attempts into spirituality. Your life is being transformed from conforming to the world, fighting satan, and being tormented by your flesh to living by faith, having a flourishing relationship with God, filling your life with the fruit of righteousness, and bearing fruit for God.

While faith is the vehicle on the other side of the needle, Jesus is still the driver. Your faith will continue to be challenged and changed as you walk with God. What you ideally would like in your walk with Christ may be filled with many faith opportunities. Psalm 126:5-6 gives a very descriptive picture of living by faith:

Those who sow in tears will reap with songs of joy. He who goes out weeping, carrying seed to sow, will return with songs of joy, carrying sheaves with him. (NIV)

The faith opportunities you face living on the other side of the needle will often result from hardships, difficulties, challenges, and dangers. Believing God and stepping out in faith may be difficult but will result in songs of joy. Your steps of faith will often not result in songs of joy if you do not sow seed. You sow seed by listening to what God is telling you. As you hear from God, pray to see His presence in what is happening. You might ask God what part He wants you to play. Is there something God wants you to share, do, or give? In other words, instead of being a silent partner with God, you actively engage God, hear, and respond.

I recently lost my billfold. I thought of every place it might have been and worked hard to find it with no success. One last place where I thought it could be was closed and could not be contacted for two days. The morning they were to open, God impressed upon me to pray that any person in need might be blessed by the cash in my wallet. It felt like a funny prayer since that would be theft, but I felt that's what I heard God say. To my good fortune, the last place did have my billfold. Everything was in it but the cash. As I praised and thanked God for retrieving my credit cards, driver's license, and other identifications, I also prayed to bless the person who had the cash. I could have been bitter and cursed the one who took my cash, but instead I praised God for His faithfulness and generosity. After all, it was God's money!

The final part of this verse is "carrying sheaves with him." Sowing into the opportunities God gives you allows Him to bless you. God's blessings will range from benefits to you. . . to blessings for others . . . to uplifting Him. The ways of God are countless, but we know that Isaiah 55:11 is true:

> '. . .It (God's Word) will not return to Me empty, but will accomplish what I desire and achieve the purpose for which I sent it.' (NIV)

The more you sow into life by faith, the more opportunities you will have for thanking God. Seeing more of the hand of God at work will further encourage your walk in Christ. We miss so much of what God is doing because we are focused on ourselves instead of the hand of God at work. As you open your eyes more to God's work, your reasons for praise and thanksgiving will be multiplied.

Your steps of faith invite Jesus to work in your life. Your steps of faith flow out of a flourishing relationship in Christ. Your life on the other side of the needle hungers for and thrives on a deepening relationship with Christ. Ephesians 3:16-19 shows a deeply expanding relationship in Christ:

> I pray that out of His glorious riches He may strengthen you with power through His Spirit in your inner being, so that Christ may dwell in your hearts through faith. And I pray that you, being rooted and established in love, may have

power, together with all the saints, to grasp how wide and long and high and deep is the love of Christ, and to know this love that surpasses knowledge — that you may be filled to the measure of all the fullness of God. (NIV)

Your relationship with Christ led the charge of taking you through the eye of the needle. Your relationship with Christ will continue to define your Christian life on the other side, but with a slight change of emphasis. The difference is in the importance of your relationship with Christ. You can go without food for forty days, but without water for only three days. On the other side of the needle your need for spiritual nourishment is much greater. **As you totally give Christ Lordship of your life, the emphasis of your walk with Christ will go from casualness and desire for more knowledge to a deepening relationship and transformation.** This focus will not be on how much you know, but how well you know the Lord of the universe. This type of relationship allows you to know and experience the full breadth of His love. Experiencing the richness of God provides an insatiable desire to be with Jesus and intimately know Him. The disciplines that brought you into the heart of God are no longer the drivers; now your driver is your intense desire to know the face of God in Psalm 27:8-9: *My heart says of you, 'Seek His face!' Your face, LORD, I will seek. Do not hide Your face from me. (NIV)*

This change of heart towards relationship with God provides important fuel for a consistent relationship and walk with Christ. Up to this point, many Christians are like drivers of Top Fuel Funny Cars. Top Fuel Funny Cars are designed to go 1,000 feet in 3.6 seconds, while Indy 500 cars are designed to go 500 miles in 3.5 hours. The lives of these Christians are like Top Fuel Funny Cars because they are marked with sharp ups and downs. These Christians live with an unpredictability that is lacking a consistent walk with Christ; it is driven by spurts of knowledge and recommitments due to trials they have faced. Life on the other side of the needle described in Ephesians 4:14-16 is marked with greater levels of consistency and maturity:

> *Then we will no longer be infants, tossed back and forth by the waves, and blown here and there by every wind of teaching and by the cunning and craftiness of men in their deceitful scheming. Instead, speaking the truth in love, we will in all things grow up into Him who is the Head, that is, Christ. From Him the whole body, joined and held together by every supporting ligament, grows and builds itself up in love, as each part does its work. (NIV)*

Real growth in Christ flourishes on the other side of the needle. **Your walk with Christ is centered on growing and experiencing Him instead of Christ being an occasional player in your life.** Your walk in Christ is no longer affected by every obstacle in life but is built on solid ground because of the truths that you have embraced and the depth of your relationship with Jesus. 2 Samuel 22:37 shows the stability of this life: *Thou dost enlarge my steps under me, and my feet have not slipped.* (NASB) You continue to grow and mature desiring less of the world and more of God. Your heart's desires continue to align with truth, not with the ways of the world.

The process of maturity and relationship with Jesus begins to move your heart to not just being sanctified to righteousness, but loving righteousness. Loving righteousness is somewhat like a person who loves today's technology. People captivated with technology want all the different kinds of equipment and the apps, programs, and ability to utilize technology in every part of their lives. GPS is an amazing advancement for travelers and everyday people navigating destinations. The technology in the GPS is not stagnant; it continues to advance. The GPS also recommends restaurants, lodging, and attractions; warns of accidents; automatically reroutes around traffic delays; warns of police, hazards in the road, weather conditions, and roadway construction; and I am sure this is only half of what is available. People love the technology because of the convenience, cost savings, and wonderful benefits. Loving righteousness is similar. You want more of God in every way because of the wonderful benefits of righteousness. **Galatians 5:22 is not a list of laws, but the opportunity, through the Holy Spirit, to touch and experience the benefits of righteousness**:

> *But the fruit of the Spirit is love, joy, peace, patience, kindness, goodness, faithfulness, gentleness and self-control. Against such things there is no law. (NIV)*

Your experiences with righteousness are bringing you more into the heart of God and allowing you to experience more of His beauty, love, grace, and work. **Righteousness allows you to embody the full personality of God with the help of the Holy Spirit!**

The fruit of righteousness begins to seed greater levels of zeal for God and His way. Isaiah 32:17 helps you understand this: *The fruit of righteousness will be peace; the effect of righteousness will be quietness and confidence forever. (NIV)* Peacefulness, quietness, and confidence are human qualities that are yearned for deeply. Yet they are natural byproducts of righteousness. You will find the fruit of the Spirit occurring more naturally throughout your life as past equivocations with living righteously have now been replaced with a fervent desire for more of God and His righteousness. **Loving righteousness reflects your life being rooted in God, your Rock, instead of the world, which shifts as sand.**

Before going through the eye of the needle, most people live their lives like they are at war with others. This includes family problems, difficult relationships, dealing with people to get things done, people treating you unfairly, people hurting you through their actions, and institutions that drive the life out of you. Living with Christ as Lord allows you to view others quite differently. Before going through the eye of the needle, life was all about you; after going through the eye of the needle, life is about pleasing the Lord. Proverbs 16:7 teaches: *When a man's ways are pleasing to the LORD, He makes even his enemies to be at peace with him.* (*NASB*) You now live for Jesus, who died for your sins. Continuing to live for yourself will preclude placing others before yourself. As Jesus did not put His interests before yours, so you should live as Philippians 2:4 instructs: *Each of you should look not only to your own interests, but also to the interests of others.* (*NIV*) It is not about how you are affected, but the condition of another's life. It is not about right and wrong, but about the cross. If Jesus can forgive you, you can forgive another in his sinful state. **Your lens of life increasingly sees the heart of others and their value in the kingdom of God.** Your motivation is not conflict, but reconciliation. Your heart is not to be right, but for others to know and experience more of Jesus.

Your motive in life is radically changing. You are becoming the peacemaker Jesus talked about in Matthew 5:9, *'Blessed are the peacemakers, for they will be called sons of God.'* (*NIV*) Your convenience, pride, oversensitivity, and moral sense of right and wrong have moved out of the way so that the salvation and sanctification of another can be of utmost importance. This lifestyle is uncommon in today's world; it is like swimming against the waves of the ocean. Putting others first will require a strength that comes from God alone. **God works in harmony; turmoil is the spoiler of God's work.** That is why harmony is a priority in Hebrews 12:15: *See to it that no one misses the grace of God and that no bitter root grows up to cause trouble and defile many.* (*NIV*) Yes, it will take God's transforming power in your life to live this way, but submitting to the Lordship of Jesus and living life with your eyes on him will allow Him to change others as well as you.

Living life on the other side results in greater fruitfulness. Fruitfulness is critical throughout your whole life in Christ. **Fruitfulness is the consummation of knowledge and faith while relationally growing in Christ.** Bearing fruit is no longer an event, but a way of living life. Fruitfulness embodies what Christ is doing in your life. Jeremiah 17:7-8 gives an almost full description of living life on the other side:

But blessed is the man who trusts in the LORD, whose confidence is in Him. He will be like a tree planted by the water that sends out its roots by the stream. It does not fear when heat comes; its leaves are always green. It has no worries in a year of drought and <u>never fails to bear fruit</u>. (NIV)

Christ in you cannot help but bear fruit. Jesus, in Luke 8:15, describes those who live on the other side of the needle,

'But the seed on good soil stands for those with a noble and good heart, who hear the word, retain it, and by persevering produce a crop.' (NIV)

There are four components to being a good seed that bears fruit:
1. A good and noble heart. A noble heart only comes out of an intimate and passionate relationship with God. You not only desire and treasure God, but you also put Him first.
2. Ask the Holy Spirit to penetrate His Word into your heart. Do not passively hear and receive truth. Hear the Word not for knowledge and stimulation, but for transformation.
3. Retain the Word. You will not retain the truth unless you have been affected by it. Write how you can apply what God is impressing in your heart. Memorize Scriptures that God is

pressing into your life. Your retention of truth causes you to apply it, helping to assure that transformation can take place.
4. The critical element of perseverance is often missed in being fruitful. Being fruitful usually is not easy or without expense. Difficulties and roadblocks make it easy to quit, but those who persevere will be fruitful (produce a crop).

Being fruitful may be the most important ingredient to living on the other side. **Without fruitfulness, your Christian life will stagnate.** The key to maintaining your vibrancy in Christ is to allow God to continue transforming your heart, so that you can respond to His direction, and persevere for the glory of God's kingdom.

EXPERIENCING GOD AS NEVER BEFORE!

Living life on the other side puts you in a position to expect more from God. This statement is not meant to portray God as a vending machine, but to prepare you for the reality of what God is about to do by you making Him Lord of your life. Much of God's work before going through the eye of the needle was spent bringing you under His Lordship. Remember that it is difficult to cross home plate when you are spending all your time in left field.

Three things that might occur from expecting more from God are:
1. Expect to praise God more because of His increasing work in your life. Also expect to thank God more for the answered prayers you are experiencing. Allow God to reveal areas of praise during your prayer times.
2. Expect God to put you into more situations where He has work to do through you. Also expect God to give you more opportunities in which He desires to minister and serve

through you. Be sensitive to the Holy Spirit's guidance and revelation for ministry and service.
3. Expect a deeper prayer life resulting from seeing the hand of God at work in and through you. Living on the tip of the spear (Trusting God) will cause you to more fervently seek God in prayer. You will be praying for things you never thought of before. Your faith in God's sovereignty to answer prayer will embolden your prayers. The answered prayers you see will further accelerate your fervency in prayer.

All three of these areas of God's involvement in your life will result in greater blessings. Remember the analogy of living on the tip of the spear? Instead of trying to get off the spear you will be screaming "Charge!" God describes the blessings on the other side in Leviticus 26:3-4:

If you walk in My statutes and keep My commandments so as to carry them out, then I shall give you rains in their season, so that the land will yield its produce and the trees of the field will bear their fruit. (NASB)

Three blessings are talked about in this verse:
- God provides the means (rains) for blessings. Do not stop charging ahead because the means are not apparent. If God wills it, He will provide it or show an alternative. A friend recently shared how God was leading his wife and him to attend a college reunion in Tulsa. They could not see how they could afford $1,828 in plane tickets from New York. The week before the reunion, God told him to check tickets out of Dallas. He found tickets for $168 each, so he was able to take his whole family to Tulsa for $504 plus a $49 per day rental car. God provided the means for what

was not possible.
- God will take care of your needs (produce) during times of ministry and service. Do not stop charging ahead because you are concerned about your needs during these times. Each month, a group of Christians I am involved with help at a local homeless shelter. A few months ago, we fell short of food because of the large number of people going through the line. While doing people counts to determine the adequacy of our food supply, a staff person opened the line for seconds, which only made the shortage worse. Another staff person encouraged calm, saying it would be okay. Minutes later an outsider brought food to the shelter which was not only the exact food we were serving, but even from the same store, plus it was already cooked! One of the volunteers commented earlier to an upset staff person, "Not to worry. If Jesus can feed 5,000, surely he can feed an extra 30 people." God can provide for your needs. All you need to do is ask!
- God will bear fruit beyond your needs. The fruit born by God will often be beyond the blessing for which you were praying. Keep charging forward knowing that God knows your every need.

Enjoy life on the other side. God will bless you beyond your wildest dreams. You will see your life change from being pulled under in the turmoil of life to experiencing the blessings God brings from deepening your relationship with Him. God's will and purpose will become clearer so that you can move from living in limbo to God imparting blessings through you. You will shift from living in the trivial to living as an instrument for salvation in every aspect of your life. You will be God's light in this dark and lost world. You will begin to experience God's approval similar to what He expressed about Jesus in Matthew 3:17: *A voice from heaven said, 'This is My Son, whom I love; with Him I am well pleased.' (NIV)* **This is true satisfaction: living in God's pleasure!**

Praise will abound out of God's many blessings. God will be active and alive in every part of your life. Negative events, positive results, and even boring times abound in satisfaction as you experience God as life itself. God's overwhelming love and presence will uphold you while consuming all that is coming against you. You will begin to identify with David in Psalm 63:4-5:

> *I will praise You as long as I live, and in Your name I will lift up my hands. My soul will be satisfied as with the richest of foods; with singing lips my mouth will praise You. (NIV)*

You will praise God for being God rather than what He does for you. Your love for God will become inexpressible. **There is nothing better than experiencing the living God in your life.**

Life on the other side is not only characterized in blessings and praise, but by a changed landscape. The way you view life changes. In Psalm 107:35-38, you see a landscape of life that has been radically changed:

> *He turned the desert into pools of water and the parched ground into flowing springs; there He brought the hungry to live, and they founded a city where they could settle. They sowed fields and planted vineyards that yielded a fruitful harvest; He blessed them, and their numbers greatly increased, and He did not let their herds diminish. (NIV)*

One of the most amazing things on the other side is that life circumstances look different. The actual circumstances may or may not have changed, but the lens you look through makes them appear better. Before you went to the other side of the eye of the needle, you saw all of life as if looking at night through a dark lens, while now you see life as if looking during the day with a clear lens. Your interpretation of life was based on a book that was not the Bible. Instead of seeing life through the eyes of the world, you now see it through God's eternal kingdom and His wonderful love, grace, and righteousness.

Your life now stands in contrast with the world. You are no longer driven by the things of this world, but by the Gospel that saves and brings life. Your landscape for living life is not the end; it is now the medium for bringing the gospel to the lost. **Your walk through life is no longer measured by the things of this world, but by the eternal footprint you leave.** The picture God is painting in you is not adorned with the perishable, but enshrined in God's message: Godly character and His fingerprints are left by the life He lives through you.

Your life before was exhausting and devoid of real meaning. Your life in Christ is now filled with purpose, while energy abounds from the depth of your relationship with Christ. Christ's purpose in you overflows with meaning and refuge. Psalm 36:7-9 reveals how energy is found in God's refuge:

How priceless is Your unfailing love! Both high and low among men find refuge in the shadow of Your wings. They feast on the abundance of Your house; You give them drink from Your river of delights. For with You is the fountain of life; in Your light we see light. (NIV)

Refuge in this verse has a dual meaning. You find refuge first in your eternal security of knowing who you are in Christ and your eternal destiny. You also find refuge in an abiding relationship with Jesus. **Refuge here is not being curled up in the corner of a dark** room, but being enveloped in the arms of your loving Savior who has secured your salvation and your satisfaction.** You can trust God, knowing He works for the good of those who love Him. You are secure in God, knowing there is nothing in all creation that can remove you from His grip. God holds you tightly as you live life through Him. **You thrive to become less so God can become more by making Him Lord of your past, present, and future.** Live in the power and love of God, who loves you beyond your earthly comprehension.

We began our journey with Psalm 24:3: *Who may ascend the hill of the LORD? Who may stand in His holy place?* (NIV) We spent seven chapters focusing on why Jesus told the rich man he could not enter the kingdom of God. Chapter 8 culminated those seven chapters into making Jesus Lord and stepping through the eye of the needle. We concluded with Chapter 9 giving you a glimpse of the other side while living in your earthly body. **Do not close this book without ascending the hill of the Lord to taste His goodness.** You may have major areas of sin or just a few; but both rob you of God's goodness and His plan for your life. **Now is the time to be all in for Jesus.** Now is the time to put every area of your life on the table for Jesus to sanctify. Allow God to show His promises through His relationship with you. Do not be someone who reads God's promises but then drifts away and forgets what they are. **Receive His promises, submit to them, and enjoy the journey with Jesus.**

John 17:15-19: *'My prayer is not that You take them out of the world but that You protect them from the evil one. They are not of the world, even as I am not of it. Sanctify them by the truth; Your word is truth. As You sent Me into the world, I have sent them into the world. For them I sanctify Myself, that they too may be truly sanctified.'* (NIV) (Jesus praying to God for His disciples and us in the garden of Gethsemane)

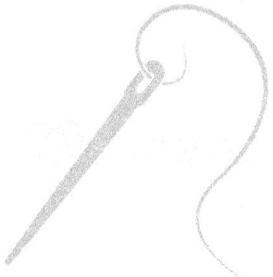

Appendix 1: The Funnel

MOVING FROM ACTIVITY TO TRANSFORMATION

Through the Eye of the Needle was written as a transformational book to take you into experiencing more of God and His work in your life. It would be easy to allow the first eight chapters to overwhelm your opportunity for transformation. To help prevent this, I have developed a simple diagram that helps collapse this book into the "Funnel Diagram." The funnel does not specify every element that prevents you from going through the eye of the needle, but it gives you a process that will help you identify hindrances and how to take those hindrances through the eye of the needle. The funnel helps you see the dynamics of your walk with Christ. This book was not written to provide you a checklist for experiencing God, but to tenderize your life to God's soft voice and leadings. As you learn to live in this position, you will start to see opportunities for God's work and presence through the illustration of the funnel. This means that as issues and opportunities arise, you will see them in light of the funnel which will provide greater clarity to the opportunity as you go down the funnel or, as the book says, through the eye of the needle. The funnel consists of six components. As issues arise you might refresh yourself on these issues from information in the book by using Appendix 3: Concordance of Topics.

Above the funnel: A large percentage of Christians live their Christian lives above the funnel where their Christian activities leave little room for God to influence or impact their lives for Christ. People in this position occasionally dip into the funnel, but they quickly

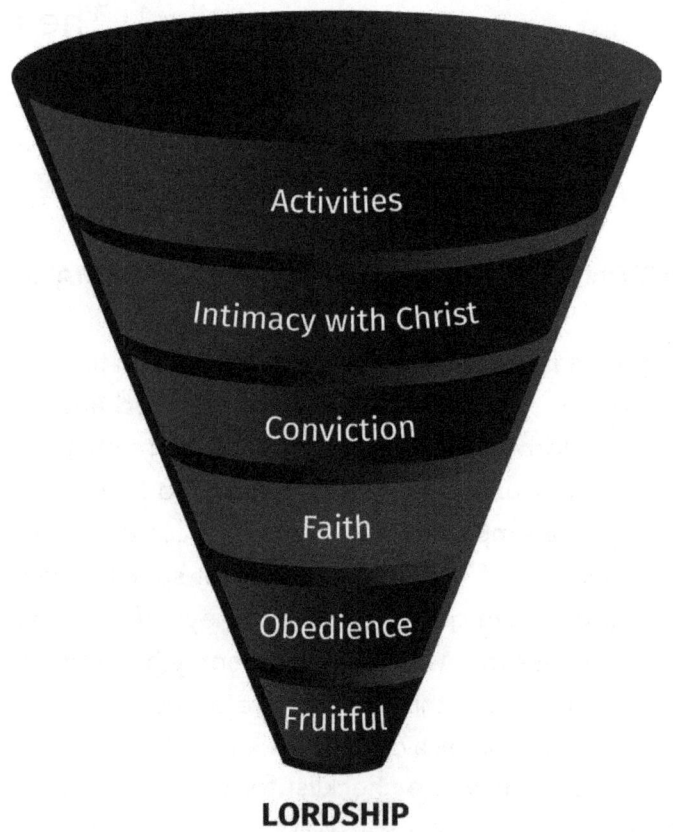

experience or reject God and withdraw to doing Christian activities. The activities provide fellowship, friendships, support groups, growth opportunities, opportunities to exercise one's giftings, intellectual stimulation, and spiritual knowledge. These are great, but not God's purpose for you. God calls Christians to be disciples who bear fruit.

Intimacy with Christ: God's number one desire is for every Christian to have a passionate and intimate relationship with Him. Many sections of the book offer suggestions in helping you have relationship with Jesus. Appendix 2: Application – Feet for Applying God's Word gives a list of additional opportunities for developing intimacy with Jesus. Everything in your Christian life will flow out of your intimacy with Christ.

Conviction: Intimacy with Christ will reveal areas of your life that need to be submitted to Christ. As you go deeper into Christ and seek to know Him better you must ask God where you need to grow, change, repent, or go. The key difference between participating in activities and applying what God is speaking is God's conviction in your heart of those areas that deprive you of God's presence, work, and fullness.

Faith: Conviction brings a crisis of faith. Do you believe and trust God enough to act? Conviction tests the boundaries and depth of your faith. Are you really willing to sacrifice, suffer, or change direction? A significant amount of the book deals with opportunities that challenge your faith. Are you willing to believe that God is bigger than the opportunities you face?

Obedience: Acting on your convictions validates your faith. Faith without obedience is dead. Faith lived out in obedience allows God to work in you.

Fruitfulness: Bearing fruit takes you through the funnel. Being fruitful is the result of obedience. Bearing fruit moves faith from talk to action. To be fruitful might take a minute or a week's worth of time. It could consist of a phone call or discipling someone each week for a year. It might be actively involved in making something happen or financially facilitating it. Whatever God is teaching, stirring, and directing in your life provides the Holy Spirit the opportunity to touch and work through you.

Make it a lifestyle to engage God throughout each day in the various activities that provide an opportunity for going through the funnel. Your life in Christ is not static, but dynamic and powerful.

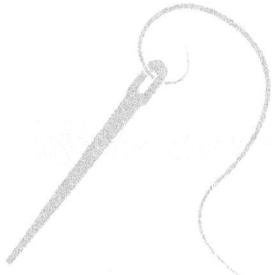

Appendix 2: Application - Feet for Applying God's Word

    This appendix is written to help you become the good soil Jesus talked about in Luke 8:15, *'But the seed on good soil stands for those with a noble and good heart, who hear the word, retain it, and by persevering produce a crop.'* (NIV) One of the best ways to make your soil richer for God is through applications. Application is taking the truths you have received from the Bible and asking God how to apply them in your life. Application is a vital element in your Christian growth and experience with Christ. The purpose of receiving Biblical truth is to allow God to touch your life. This might include God convicting you of sin in your life, direction and purpose for all areas of your life, greater intimacy with Christ, spiritual principles to deepen your faith, or structural growth to live life. Psalm 51:6 shows how application leads to truth: *You (God) desire truth in the inward being; therefore teach me wisdom in my secret heart. (NRSV)* God desires truth to be in you. The question is how this happens. It is not enough to just hear Biblical truths; allow God to transform those truths into wisdom through the application of Biblical principles. Allowing God to take you into wisdom allows Him to touch and change your heart.

The goal of application is to not miss what God desires for you. The guiding principle of application is to not allow truth that God impresses on your heart to go unaddressed. Prayerfully ask God what He would have you do to better walk with Him and serve Him. I call the methods of application "feet" because they take you into the heart of God and what He desires for you. Feet can be any number of activities that open your life more to God's presence, work, and direction. The following are some feet I have developed in my 47-year walk with Christ. This list is provided to illustrate things that can be done to apply God's Word. You may have more, less, different, or the same modifications. What you do will be born out of prayer and what works for you. Your goal is to hear God and provide the feet that allow you to best live out your life in and for Christ. James 1:22 challenges you to obey the Word: *Do not merely listen to the Word, and so deceive yourselves. Do what it says. (NIV)*

FEET FOR APPLYING GOD'S WORD

1. Daily – Journal an application from your daily quiet time. What is one thing God pressed upon your heart during your time with Him? Transcribe only that portion of the Scripture that applies to your application to help you easily reference God's Word. Make the application brief so that it is not a laborious exercise. Journaling allows you to easily look back over time at how God has spoken to you. It will also keep you focused on listening and responding each day as you meet with God. In Mark 1:35 Jesus sets the pattern for the

daily quiet time: *Very early in the morning, while it was still dark, Jesus got up, left the house and went off to a solitary place, where He prayed.* (NIV)

2. Daily - Memorize Scriptures God has impressed on you for application. Scripture memory provides one of the best ways to allow God's transformative work in you. Set up a review schedule for those Scriptures +you have memorized. Allow God to sculpt your life as you meditate on His Word. Devote some of your dead time (while in your car stuck in traffic or at stop lights, waiting for an appointment, waiting in line) for Scripture memory. This is a habit that takes little time, but produces great benefits.

3. Weekly - Review seven days of applications from the past week's quiet times to allow God to continue to touch your heart with them. I prefer Sunday morning. Give God a second chance to press you where He is leading you. Watch for patterns of impression that God might be leading you into from the past week's applications. Meditate on what God has been teaching you.

4. Weekly – On an ongoing basis, compile a list of major applications for areas of your life where God desires a major emphasis, change, or growth. Applications may include humility, witnessing, serving, purity, etc. In the last twenty years, God has given me 38 major applications.

5. Quarterly – Develop applications for any formal Bible Study you do by asking these questions: What impressed me? Where do I fall short? What by the grace of God am I going to do about it? Review specific applications from each study, each quarter, by reviewing one set of study applications each week until you have reviewed all your study applications. Develop the life habit of not just studying the Bible, but allowing God to impact your life by applying His Word.

Allow God to use the applications from the Bible Studies you have done to help you develop greater spiritual intimacy with Him, grow in Christlikeness, and be impacted to serve and minister in greater measures.

6. Develop applications from the books you read. These applications can be applied in any of the ways already discussed. You can also develop your own personal concordance by topic. What you read is quite often where God is working. Make it easy to refresh yourself.

7. Bi-annually - Use the applications from all your sources of truth to develop a "Life Plan" for all the areas of your life. Plot various applications in the appropriate areas of your Life Plan: spiritual, marriage, children, vocation, personal and so on. Tie specific applications that correspond to the plan God is developing for your life. Review twice a year for update, challenge, and accountability. Your life plan will include a combination of applications as well as activities and goals. Not every goal will be accentuated with a Scripture or application.

8. Utilize computerized calendars to remind you to pray for areas of your life (applications) where God is leading you or pressing into you.

9. Memorize Scripture strategically:
(a) Memorize in areas of your life that God is cultivating: Anger, purity, being judgmental, selfishness and so on.
(b) Memorize in areas that God is leading you in ministry and service such as serving the poor, fighting for the life of the unborn, etc.

None of these activities take much time if you organize them in a way that spreads them out. That way they are not burdensome, but enjoyable and enriching. Make them a life habit.

Allow God to use your feet for making the soil of your life richer. Your Feet will be the activities God has cultivated in your life for allowing His maximum expression of His life through you. These are not required to live a full Christian life; but if God is good, why wouldn't you pursue Him as diligently as you would pursue a passion of this world? God will use the feet you adopt to help you experience more of Him as well as allow Him to maximize all He has for you. In life you apply yourself to what you want: vocation, sports, hobbies, family. Why would you do less with God than you do with the things of this world? What you do will ultimately flow out of your love and passion for Him. Your God is truly worthy of all of your love and passion.

> *Colossians 3:23-24: Whatever you do, work at it with all your heart, as working for the Lord, not for men, since you know that you will receive an inheritance from the Lord as a reward. It is the Lord Christ you are serving. (NIV)*

The **Growing in Christ** website (www.growinginchrist.net) contains Bible studies that detail how to do many of the activities mentioned. Journaling applications is covered in "Your Life in Christ," "Deeper With God," and "Transformation – Part 1." "Discipleship: One-on-One" provides a good teaching on Scripture memory. There are other studies that may also be helpful on better applying the content of this book. The Bible Study, "Satisfaction," will directly help you in applying the principals of *Through the Eye of the Needle*.

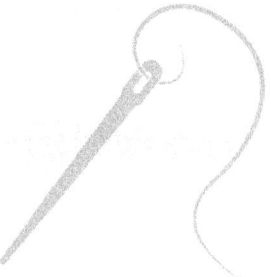

Appendix 3: Concordance of Topics

BECOMING LESS, SO THAT JESUS CAN BECOME MORE

Through the Eye of the Needle was not written to incrementally enhance a Christian's walk, but to fundamentally transform a Christian's life into a completely devoted follower of Christ. Taking hold of Christ and making Him Lord over everything fundamentally changes your walk with Christ. This concordance will help you easily access key topics in which you desire further study and meditation for growth and transformation.

It also provides a library of short teachings that you can use not only in your life, but also in the lives of those with whom you have the opportunity to minister. Seldom did a week go by during the writing process of this book where I did not use a section of this book to help another person. The topics are alphabetically identified by chapter and subheading to help you access the needed information.

You can find the read on the topic by going to the identified chapter and then finding the subtitle for the section written on the topic.

LIBRARY OF HELPFUL TEACHINGS

Bigger God: Chapter 3 – Introduction
Blocking God: Chapter 5 – Introduction
Desiring Transformation: Chapter 1 – Introduction
Carnal living: Chapter 7 – Within Whose Kingdom Do You Reside?
Commitment: Chapter 2 – Position 10 – Committed Heart
Compromise: Chapter 5 – Big, Bad Self
Complacency: Chapter 2 – Position 6 – Complacency
Control: Chapter 3 – Owned by God
Corrupted Beliefs: Chapter 1 – Salvation
Culture: Chapter 2 – Position 8 – Lordship
Die to Self: Chapter 3 – Die to Self
Eternal Security: Chapter 2 – Position 1 – Knowing Christ as Lord and Savior
Exchanged Life: Chapter 9 – Introduction
Experiencing Christ: Your evaluation: Chapter 1 – Introduction
Experiencing Christ: Chapter 6 – Experiencing Christ
Experiencing Christ: Chapter 8 – Living Out of the Fruit of Righteousness
Experiencing Christ: Chapter 9 – Experiencing Christ as Never Before
Faith: Chapter 1 – Childlike Faith
Faith: Chapter 3 – Take Your Position
Faith: Chapter 4 – Positioning Like a Child

Appendix

Faith: Chapter 7 – Divine or Human?
Fear of God: Chapter 3 – Fearing God
Finding God: Chapter 3 – Seeking and Waiting on God
Forgiveness: Chapter 5 – Capturing the Future
Fruitful: Chapter 2 – Position 4 – The Soils of Your Life
Fruitful: Chapter 2 – Position 5 – Bearing Fruit for God
Fruitful: Chapter 9 – Your Life on the Other Side of the Needle
God's Love: Chapter 3 – Knowing God's Love
God's Magnificence: Chapter 3 – Our Incomparable, Incomprehensible, Wonderful God
Grace: Chapter 1 – Threading the Needle with Grace
Growing: Chapter 6 – Feeding the Heart
Hard Heart: Chapter 2 – Position 9 – Hard Heart
Heart for God: Chapter 6 – Introduction
Holy Spirit: Chapter 8 – Empowered by the Holy Spirit
Humility: Chapter 4 – Positioning in Humility
Humility: Chapter 6 – A Heart for People
Identity in Christ: Chapter 9 – Your Position on the Other Side of the Needle
Idols: Chapter 5 – God's Gold
Let Go, Let God: Chapter 8 – Introduction
Living the Christian Life: Chapter 9 – Your Life on the Other Side of the Needle
Lordship: Chapter 1 – Threading the Needle – Make Jesus Lord
Lordship: Chapter 2 – Position 2 – Who's on Base
Lordship: Chapter 2 – Position 8 – Lordship
Lordship: Chapter 4 – Positioned by Being Sold Out
Lordship: Chapter 5 – Make Jesus Lord
Lordship: Chapter 6 – Jesus' Heart
Lordship: Chapter 7 – God's Way
Lordship: Chapter 7 – Within Whose Kingdom Do You Reside?
Lordship: Chapter 7 – Choosing God

Loving God: Chapter 3 – Delight in the Lord
Loving God: Chapter 6 –- A Heart for God
Maturity in Christ: Chapter 1 – Threading the Needle by Growing to Maturity
Mindset of Christ: Chapter 1 – Introduction
Obedience: Chapter 7 – Introduction
Obedience: Chapter 8 – Living in Obedience
Peace: Chapter 6 - Peace
Persevering: Chapter 2 – Position 3 – Pursuing Jesus
Picture of a Christian: Chapter 2 – Position 11 – A Satisfied Heart
Positioning for God: Chapter 4 – Introduction
Pride: Chapter 5 – Big, Bad Self
Relationship with Jesus: Chapter 1 – Threading the Needle by Knowing Him
Releasing Christ: Chapter 5 – Do I Love Righteousness?
Repentance: Chapter 1 – Threading the Needle with Grace
Righteous Living: Chapter 4 – Positioning for Righteousness
Righteousness: Chapter 1 – Threading the Needle with Righteousness
Righteousness: Chapter 2 – Position 7 – Righteousness
Righteousness: Delighting in – Chapter 6 – A Heart for Righteousness
Righteousness: Chapter 7 – Loving Righteousness More Than the World
Salvation: Chapter 1 – Your Foundation
Salvation: Chapter 1 – Threading the Needle – Salvation
Salvation: Chapter 2 – Position 1 – Knowing Christ as Savior
Sanctification: Chapter 7 – Loving Righteousness More Than the World
Servanthood: Chapter 4 – Positioned by Being Last
Serving: Chapter 4 – Positioned by Serving
Stagnation: Chapter 2 – Position 6 – Complacency

Appendix

Sufficiency: Chapter 5 – Big, Bad Self
Sustainer: Chapter 4 – Positioning God as My Sustainer
Transformation: Chapter 1 – Threading the Needle – Transformation
Trusting God: Chapter 3 – Absolute Trust
Trusting God: Chapter 8 – Anchor to Jesus
Trusting God: Chapter 7 – Within Whose Kingdom Do You Reside?
Trust Issues: Chapter 5 – Trust Busters
Victorious living: Chapter 9 – Your Position on the Other Side of the Needle
Waiting on God: Chapter 4 – Positioning by Waiting on God
Will – Shaping: Chapter 7 – Introduction
Witnessing: Chapter 6 – Upgrade for Free

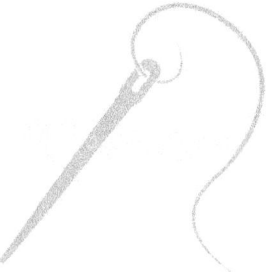

Special Thanks

Overwhelming heartfelt thanks goes to God the Father who is the real author of *Through the Eye of the Needle.* All praise and thankfulness go to God for the miracle of His life in all who believe.

I owe a debt of love and gratitude to my wife, Libbi, who's tireless challenging, editing, and valuable insights greatly shaped the finished work. Her work, support, and understanding helped make this book happen.

My special thanks to my daughters, Kristen Holmes and Alison Berger, as well as my son-in-law, Thomas Berger, who were constantly available with opinions and ideas for various aspects of the book. Their insight and support helped supplement my deficiencies while offering quality suggestions that further improved the book.

Countless friends gave critical reviews and suggestions during the writing and editing process. Special thanks go to Linda Smiley, Kathy Buffington, Brad Moore, and Debbie Huff who made significant contributions chapter by chapter. Their editing, review, and clarity contributed greatly to this work.

About Charles T. Davis

Charles T. Davis has worked in the business field for 44 years and served the Lord in ministry, in business, and in life. During his business career, he worked in sales and sales management, led a $200 million company as president for 18 years, and developed his own consulting business with customers in 42 states and two foreign countries.

While going through school and during his working career, he held church leadership positions for youth, taught Sunday school, and presided over multiple Bible study groups. He received training in conferences held by Campus Crusade, Navigators, Truth Project, CBMC, Episcopal Divinity School, and many others. He has a degree in Ethical and Religious Studies from the University of Oklahoma. Passionately walking with Christ daily in a consistent fashion has given him a zeal for sharing and teaching the Word of God.

In 1995, Charles began an active program of discipling men one-on-one. He began writing Bible studies because he found a need for accessible, inexpensive, easily-transferable, topical Bible Studies to support Christians in their daily walk with Christ. While continuing to operate his consulting business, he developed the website Growinginchrist.net where he offers his work, which includes over 112 Bible lessons in 22 topical Bible studies and 500 devotions. His driving passion is that these Bible studies, devotions, and *Through the Eye of the Needle* will help every Christian experience the fullness and purpose of Christ.

www.ingramcontent.com/pod-product-compliance
Lightning Source LLC
LaVergne TN
LVHW092316080426
835509LV00034B/237